S0-DZH-383

# THE THEORY AND PRACTICE OF COMMUNICATING EDUCATIONAL AND VOCATIONAL INFORMATION

ANN M. MARTIN

INDIANA STATE UNIVERSITY

HOUGHTON MIFFLIN COMPANY · BOSTON

NEW YORK · ATLANTA · GENEVA, ILL. · DALLAS · PALO ALTO

Library of Congress Catalog Card
Number: 70–129169

ISBN: 0–395–09939–0

COPYRIGHT © 1971 BY HOUGHTON MIFFLIN COMPANY. *All rights
reserved. No part of this work may be reproduced or transmitted
in any form or by any means, electronic or mechanical, including
photocopying and recording, or by any information storage or retrieval
system, without permission in writing from the publisher. Printed
in the U.S.A.*

LB
1028
371.4       .m28
M363t

125606

# CONTENTS

135114

# EDITORS' INTRODUCTION

The author of this monograph has sought to describe, without becoming bogged down in minutia, the theory and practice of communicating educational and vocational information to students. The focus of both theory and practice is upon individuals as they interact with others and with their environment; further, it is upon how, when, and why they seek and utilize information.

A fundamental premise underlying communication of educational and vocational information is that such information will enable the individual to make sound decisions—sound for himself and for society. The author makes the point in a most telling way that the goal in communicating information is always to enable the student to be more effective in dealing with his present and future environments and more confident about himself. Achievement of a more meaningful and productive integration of self and situation is an outcome of such a process.

This monograph stresses the importance of experimentation and innovation in the informational service and the necessity for developing improved techniques for processing and communicating information. In this connection, the author, Ann Martin, draws upon the research to illuminate theory and practice. There can be little doubt that new and increased demands are being made upon the informational service to play a fuller role in making guidance programs stronger and more meaningful.

SHELLEY C. STONE

BRUCE SHERTZER

# AUTHOR'S INTRODUCTION

This monograph has been written from a distinct point of view. It is evident that I think that the guidance function, which includes the communication of vocational information, should be based on theory and practice that permit a *humanistic* approach to the growth, development, and change of the individual. The argument as to whether or not guidance is a discipline which can have a theory of its own has not been directly tackled in this book. Perhaps it is too early to say. Although various vocational theorists have provided models of career development which must be recognized in the total schema, it is evident that I am currently convinced that they are operational only in terms of their applicability to psychological and sociological theory.

The first three chapters are devoted primarily to theoretical concerns, and the latter three to practical concerns. These two sections may be read independently, although I do not think that this is advisable. I think that to read one section without the other would be like trying in the first instance to deal with form without substance and in the second instance to deal with substance without form.

Chapter 1 reviews the current developments in education that have resulted in a closer relationship between educational and vocational concerns. Several major implications for making the curriculum more functional are then discussed. Chapters 2 and 3 ask what principles of guidance apply in effecting growth and change in view of these recent developments. This question can only be answered with consideration of: (1) Whom do we want to change and why; (2) What is the nature of the change we are going to make; and (3) What are the means of effecting change. The dichotomy presented is between learning formulations that lend themselves to the technology of mechanistic guidance systems and new formulations of complex forms of learning (cognitive and affective) that lend themselves to the technology of humanistic guidance systems.

The practical concerns of communicating information and promoting change through guidance are then considered. Emphasis is placed on the necessity for the practitioner to identify guidance materials and procedures that fit into a developmental approach and that can be used to penetrate and re-form the curriculum in the humanistic interest of the individual child.

Like all such undertakings, this monograph represents the joint efforts of many individuals. The author's debt is manifold. There is my debt to those whose conceptions and researches have been drawn upon and presented in these pages. There is my debt to numerous colleagues who over a period of years greatly broadened and strengthened my knowledge and perspective in relation to the underlying concern of this book. My debt is particularly great to Maurice F. X. Donohue, Ralph Boynton, Theodore Conant, and Robert Rosenthal. There is my debt to graduate students, Betty Alty Crafts, Sandra Days, and Leon Raesly, whose many, many hours of help and assistance are gratefully acknowledged. There is a special note of appreciation from their devoted boss to two former assistants, Madelaine Spinello and Elaine Roehling. A special note of thanks is due Marcia G. Arnold, who assisted in the preparation of this monograph and was responsible for reading and editing the manuscript. Her interest and skill contributed greatly to the finished product. Thanks is also due to Maryalys Melvin for her patience in typing the manuscript.

Finally, there is an enormous debt to A. W. Bendig, who prevented the author from being a graduate school dropout; Marc Matland, from the USOE, who believed in the idea from the first; and Ed Roeber, who provided the author "high ground" so that this book could be written.

The book is dedicated to my mother and father.

ANN M. MARTIN

# The Changing Character
# of Education

In order to delineate a guidance information program of materials and techniques relevant to the educational process, it is necessary to discuss the changes that are gradually evolving in education today. This first chapter is not intended to be complete in detail with respect to these innovations, as such an effort would be pretentious and beyond the scope of this monograph. Additionally, there has been little concurrence on specific details of appropriate educational change among those of differing philosophies and beliefs. For our purposes it is sufficient to comment upon new patterns in the character of education that have significance for the development and use of new guidance media and techniques. Thus, the introductory material presented in this chapter is designed to provide a coherent background against which to read and interpret the theoretical and technological developments that are occurring with respect to the guidance function as reported in the chapters that follow.

### Synthesis of Vocational Preparation and General Education

In the decade following Sputnik (1957), *quality* in education was interpreted as meaning an excellent preparation for collegiate study for students who clearly demonstrated academic promise in the early grades. Discipline areas were fundamental, and curriculum reform movements, evident in the years following World War II, became vastly accelerated — notably in mathematics and the physical sciences. Youth had to be taught selected content elements in highly specialized and technical areas to fit into a professional occupational structure that was changing at a rapidly increasing pace. During this period, curriculum revision groups (e.g., SMSG, PSSC, PSCS) focused their efforts on the precollegiate program, thus embracing primarily the college-bound student (Goodlad, 1966). What was neglected in these efforts, however, was the fact that the largest proportion of our American youth does not enter or complete a college program. Socioeconomic, ethnic, and geographic discrimination presented subtle yet systematic impediments to the educational progress of noncollege-bound youth, yet these barriers were scarcely voiced in the early period of curriculum reform (Conant, 1961).

During the past five or six years it has become patently clear that American education is faced with a problem of alarming proportions. How could this system of modern education that many point to as one of the primary achievements of our culture fail to recognize the needs of "the other fifty percent" (Super, 1964)? Large numbers of graduates who do not go to college are leaving high school totally lacking in any of the requisite skills or abilities required in our complex society today. These graduates are drifting passively and haphazardly into minimum-skill, and rapidly disappearing jobs; an increasing proportion are headed toward extended unemployment or uncertain and unsatisfying work lives. The majority of these graduates have given little thought to a career line which might increase job satisfaction and self-fulfillment in the real and constantly changing job market (U.S. Dept. of Labor, 1966).

Faced with these concerns, the Federal government has moved to provide increased allocations of public funds for specialized and vocational programs in and beyond high school and at the noncollegiate levels. Significant legislation resulted (Vocational Education Act of 1963), enabling curriculum reform to take place not only in academic subject areas but throughout the entire structure of general and vocational education. Specifically, the philosophy was that schools should move toward a model of general vocational education which would not be subsidiary to, but part of, a comprehensive high school program.

To facilitate this premise, the U.S. Office of Education proposed a model vocational-educational curriculum that could in theory be closely integrated with the standard school curricula at all levels of instruction. This model would put into operation many of the recommendations and conclusions of the Venn study (1964) of the place of occupational education within education as a whole and within the nation's new technological economy.

As a result, many school systems in small as well as large metropolitan areas made active commitments to the total reorganization of their schools in order to provide for the development and installation of new types of curricular approaches to vocational education and guidance. This new approach was designated as "An Educational System for the 70's" and was to be developed with the administrative and technical assistance of a consortium of schools throughout the nation (Bushnell, 1968). The System's design was based on Morgan and Bushnell's (1968) concept of an *organic curriculum* which is, in essence, a system of general vocational instruction set within a developmental framework incorporating strategies for new instructional approaches and techniques. In general, Morgan and Bushnell proposed that the overall design of this curriculum should:

1. Integrate academic and vocational learning by appropriately employing vocational preparation as one of the principal vehicles for the inculcation of basic learning skills. In this way learning could be made more palatable to many students who otherwise would have difficulty seeing the value of a general education.

2. Expose the student to an understanding of the "real world" through a series of experiences which capitalizes on the desire of youth to investigate for himself.

3. Train the student in a core of generalizable skills related to a cluster of occupations rather than just those related to one specialized occupation.

4. Orient students to the attitudes and habits which go with successful job performance and successful living.

5. Provide a background for the prospective worker by helping him to understand how he fits within the economic and civic institutions of our country.

6. Make students aware that learning is life-oriented and need not, indeed must not, stop with the exit from formal education.

7. Help students cope with a changing world of work through developing career strategies which can lead to an adequate level of income and responsibility.

8. Create within the student a sense of self-reliance and awareness which leads him to seek out appropriate careers with realistic aspiration levels.

Each local school district was to carefully examine and analyze its own structure in terms of requirements so that changes and revisions instituted would make the program meaningful for its own area and pertinent to the characteristics of its student body.

## Job Clusters and Job Ladders

A major departure from the customary principles of vocational education is the *cluster* concept. Theoretically, the concept when operational should provide flexibility for the individual in his future vocational life. Designed to prepare the student for a specific job such as plumber or key punch operator, the traditional vocational program neglects to recognize the need for flexibility within a field of related occupations. The *cluster* concept is specifically aimed at the development of skills and knowledges (capabilities) common to a variety of occupations in a given field, thus preparing the student to move freely among a family of occupations (i.e., health related occupations, research laboratory occupations, machine trade occupations, etc.).

It should be recognized that problems exist in defining what constitutes the basic skills and knowledge. Although thinking in this area is still at a rudimentary level, practitioners agree that these capabilities should include the development of learning techniques basic to the acquisition of additional knowledge and skills and the ability to apply these techniques to new or novel problem solving situations. It has finally been acknowledged that these skills and capabilities go well beyond the academic skills of reading, writing, and arithmetic.

Work on defining jobs in related occupational areas has also been conducted by the U.S. Employment Service as set forth in the Third Edition of the Dictionary of Occupational Titles (DOT). Their efforts have been primarily directed toward greater flexibility in personnel practices of recruitment, selection, and placement.

A related concept that has significance for vocational education and guidance is the concept of *job ladders*. Here the aim is to enable less skilled workers to start off in entry occupations and then give them a chance to move up as they gain education and skill. This may sound simple and sensible, but it is really a revolutionary idea that is only beginning to receive attention. At present, it is difficult for a worker to progress from a service to a semiprofessional and on to a professional occupation — i.e., from nurse's aide to practical nurse to registered nurse. Girls are now expected to start at the beginning in meeting educational and other requirements for each of these occupations. Utilizing the job ladder concept, credit for training and experience as a nurse's aide would be applied toward the requirements for practical nursing and so on up the ladder toward the requirements for professional nursing. Implementation of this educational crediting system is difficult to achieve because of traditional institutional barriers. Hospital education councils are working on the problem and the result could be helpful in decreasing personnel shortages in these occupations, in addition to benefiting many women who were not in a position to train initially for a professional career. Teaching, counseling, social work, and library work are examples of other fields where there are personnel shortages and where increased efforts are being made to open opportunities for subprofessional personnel.

In summary, we now see attempts among industry, labor, and professional societies to interact in an effort committed to the redesigning of jobs and the restructuring of career ladders with the initial intent to absorb all workers into vocational areas regardless of skill level. In conjunction with these efforts, vocational education must translate the requirements of these newly designed jobs and job ladders to the education and training demands placed on the school system. With this in mind, the educational system must be geared to produce graduates at various levels of formation; guidance as an inherent function of the system must provide a process mechanism whereby all individuals can be aided in achieving continuous progress toward a wide range of vocational opportunities.

## Toward A Functional Curriculum

The major change of note in curriculum development in our comprehensive school is that curricular goals for public school systems, once tied to arbitrary academic standards, are now becoming tied to more functional criteria of school achievement and success. In effect, the question that is currently being raised is, What has the student learned and what is he able to do no matter where he exits from the curriculum?

Functional criteria call for the introduction into the educational program of the following steps: (1) individual assessment of stage of learning and academic skills; (2) development of a plan for next step of learning and implementation of plan; and (3) evaluation of what is learned and repeat of cycle. It is to be anticipated that there are students for whom motivation to move up the functional "ladder" must be provided.

In response to the changes, primarily qualitative (i.e., changes in character), that are taking place in education and on the work front, educational objectives are becoming increasingly concerned with what each individual child can do *now* rather than whether or not he measures up to an arbitrary academic standard in some reliable or valid way. This change in the nature of the objectives of education is reflected by the procedure for assessment of achievement adopted by the National Assessment Program. What constitutes a "score" in their evaluation of American school children is whether a student can or cannot perform any given task (a pass-fail criterion of success) rather than how the individual excels in that task compared to the rest of the group. In other words, the primary concern is with what the student can do or cannot do rather than how well he stacks up against his peers.

It has been said by leading educators that the objectives of education are "becoming more humble" as education readjusts its programs to reach the larger proportion of American youth. The most important feature of this process is the necessity of providing a specific plan for the individual student that is based on his particular requirements. Now that the potential of new teaching methods and technology for individualization is recognized, it can, we trust, be applied successfully to meet the demands of these emerging objectives.

This increased concern for the vocational development of each and every student in our society requires the practitioner to re-evaluate the methods and objectives of vocational guidance and counseling. This creates new demands on school administrators, curriculum specialists, teachers, and counselors, requiring them to (1) think in terms of new programs that bring education and work into a more direct relationship; (2) gain a new perspective on education and their responsibility for its relevancy; and (3) become concerned with where students are in their vocational development, where they should go next and, then, how they are going to get there.

As a result of this changed emphasis and concern, guidance as a function is coming into its own. In the last ten years the number of guidance counselors in elementary and secondary schools has more than tripled. Traditional guidance processes are being examined, old ones redesigned, and new ones created. Thus, as a result of the changing character of education, the whole area of guidance — its concepts, procedures, and processes — is undergoing review and development.

# Guidance Objectives in Information Processing Systems Design

Two developments of note are taking place in education and guidance in response to the obligation of dealing with the individual in the changing school environment. The first is the design of "Vocational Information Processing Systems" and the introduction of systems concepts into vocational and career guidance (Perrone and Thrush, 1969). The second is the preparation of novel types of communications media and techniques to reach students with different psychological and sociological make-ups. These developments are of special significance for the selection and use of educational and vocational information by guidance specialists.

The introduction of systems concepts to occupational information and vocational guidance was, in the author's opinion, adventitious, yet it resulted in positive outcomes. First, the development of "Vocational Information Processing Systems" should prove most valuable to educational-vocational counselors searching the effective media for communicating certain guidance concepts and information. Second, the systems approach, by its very nature, requires a precise description of the operations which the system is to perform analogous to operations presently being performed in the real world. This allows the counselor to compare and evaluate the goals, objectives, and procedures of his own vocational information guidance program and practice with the goals, objectives, and procedures of the model systems currently being devised. More than an academic exercise, this activity requires the counselor to think through and to make explicit for himself the decisions he has made for the selection and use of guidance materials and procedures. But this exercise is one that is too commonly ignored.

In designing information systems (or a set of manual procedures) for the use of educational and vocational information, important judgments must be made with regard to the *goals* and *purposes* of the information system and the *means* that the system will use to reach its stated objectives. Further, these judgments should always take into account the nature of the audience served by the system. In the course of making a vocational information system operational, the designer should be engaged in three major decisions that determine (1) the nature of the change to be made; (2) whom the system will change and why; and (3) how the system will bring about change. The three basic decisions enumerated above will now be considered in greater depth with examples.

### The Nature of the Change to be Made

There is probably general agreement that the provision of educational and vocational information is not to be considered a single event but rather as part of a long-term program and continuing process. This is particularly true in view of the present theoretical emphasis of Ginsburg et al. (1951), Super (1953, 1957), and Tiedemann and O'Hara (1963) regarding the developmental nature of vocational decisions. Differences that occur in the practice and use of educational and vocational information generally stem from divergent beliefs on the part of the counselor regarding the nature of the individual as a human being and a processor of information. Let us illustrate this discussion by analyzing two distinct points of view of the counselee and examine the extent to which these views result in differences in actual practice. One view and its implications for the overall use of information will then be pursued in greater detail.

On the one hand, the guidance counselor often proceeds as though the counselee were a rational data processing machine. In this instance, he behaves as though all that the student requires is to have his "deficit" of information filled by providing him with appropriate facts — both oral and printed. When the counselee is treated in this manner, the assumption is that facts make the individual more knowledgeable and wise, and provide plans and direction to goals. In the course of his duties and responsibilities, the counselor identifies usable techniques to match students, information, and goals to determine what the individual needs or does not need to know. This viewpoint has led to increased emphasis on the refinement of educational and vocational information to make it more objective and factual. Undoubtedly, there are times when a little objective or factual information is all that is required. Unfortunately, the foregoing philosophy and approach tends to make each use of information a separate and isolated event based on the immediacy of the acknowledged deficit.

When the information system designer observes the individual as being a rational sensate machine and recognizes his main duty as dealing with the provision of facts in the vocational development of the child, he will structure the system one way; but when he views the individual as being a complex human being with emotions, knowledge, perceptions, and prejudices, he will structure the system in a different manner. Let us now examine this second philosophy and approach.

Psychological studies of perception have repeatedly indicated that predisposed attitudes, emotional states, and past experiences govern the individual's perception, distortion, and selection of various types of input data. Borow has been instrumental in directing the attention of the counseling profession to these affective variables (1964, 1966). The counselor who looks at the implications of these findings proceeds to assess the individual's stage of perception and awareness to determine whether the individual must first be counseled on affective grounds before providing a process of cognitive information. In the early stages of vocational counseling with adolescents, a great deal of the change to take place in the individual requires a change in affect. In considering the utility of information for change the counselor looks toward a different set of procedures than he would use if he were attempting to fill a "deficit" or produce an increment in knowledge. These procedures call for determining what common affective problems of vocational choice and decision may face the student and how individualized the responses (choices) will be. The emphasis will be on the *chooser* who makes his choice out of the context of his complexity as a human being.

This second approach has led to increased concern with a method for the recognition of emotional impediments and thereby opens the way to overcome these impediments to utilization of information. If this is so, this new method must reduce the discomfort that comes from focusing on emotional aspects while the individual develops mechanisms and techniques to establish new motivational patterns and goals.

When dealing with affective behavior the counselor must recognize that a process of unlearning must take place in order to reduce the intensity of affective feelings. In dealing with unlearning, the counselor should attempt to motivate the individual to: (1) clarify his own behavior in relation to that of others in terms of his attitudes, values, and expectations; (2) proceed to strengthen the voluntary control of his social behavior; and (3) seek out and expand knowledge and skills relevant to himself and his goals. These three essential objectives to be achieved by each student in the course of his unlearning and change will be carefully reviewed below.

### The Student Must Respond with the Truth

The initial objective in the student's exploration of attitudes, values, and expectations in the interests of unlearning, growth, and change is the recognition that he must respond to the information system with the way he feels. He must tell the truth, which is his perception of reality. This may sound like a simple statement, yet the practitioner knows that he must continually remind himself that youth generally expect to get "punished" for telling the truth. The statement "I hate my mother" has not yet received general acceptance. So the practitioner finds himself hard pressed to devise a means for the system to prove to the student that he will not be punished for telling the truth.

Cronbach (1969) provides us with a good example of the concern about the student's reaction to a machine system in his recent article on whether a machine can "fit" an applicant to continuing education.

> As long as the student is fighting for his future standard of living he will tell the computer what he thinks the computer wants to hear. Questions that would be entirely appropriate in an instructional setting become invasions of privacy and acts of arrogance when the computer (or anyone else) threatens to pass judgement on a student in terms of whether it likes his values.

Practical evidence indicates that the student usually responds not as one person but as three: the *socialized self;* the *idealized self;* the *feared* or *despised self.* Realizing this, the counselor can gradually make the student aware that in telling the truth, he generally reacts with one of these three separate sets of responses with respect to statements of goals, values, and motives. But which of the three is responding? Is it the one who has been taught or has learned to respond the way he thinks he is expected to respond — the *socialized self?* Is it the one who responds the way he thinks a person whom he really admires and who really loves him wants or expects him to respond — the *idealized self?* Or is it the one who responds the way he thinks those who dislike him and really know his weaknesses would expect him to respond — the *feared* or *despised self?*

The counselor and the student must come to discover that in dealing with the truth they are working with three separate sets of perceptions, and they must be aware of which of these three is operating in the course of communication.

### The Student Must Recognize Disturbances in His Own Social Behavior

A second significant objective in the student's exploration of attitudes, values, and expectations in the interests of unlearning, growth, and change is that he recognize symptom patterns in his own social behavior. All freedom is contagious and if the student gets to the point where he can tell the truth and recognize it as such, he will probably want to act the way he feels. For example, he may think about dropping out of school, destroying school or community property, or engaging in isolating behaviors. The youth, with the help of the counselor, teacher, and other guidance personnel within his social radius, must be assisted to resolve such emerging social crises. To aid the student, the guidance program can do two things: (1) it can provide simulated situations or role play in which the student can explore his feelings and his projected actions and their consequences, and (2) it can provide information and social models that will enable the student to learn how to be rational in order to confront a rational world. The information and activities must be designed to enable the student to understand that emphasis on the rational will permit him to be more objective and effective and thus in a better position to realize his intentions.

### The Student Must Develop Cognitive Goals

To aid the student in his search for rationality, it is essential that he be led to acquire not only an awareness of *self*, but also of certain concepts, principles, and rules that will enable him to recognize the dynamics of the social institutions and society in which he lives and to project himself with some appropriate perspective into a variety of adult and work roles. Hopefully, these concepts, principles, and rules will provide the stuff with which the student will think in mastering the process skills of planning, problem-solving, and decision-making. Therefore, a final major objective in the student's exploration of attitudes, values, and expectations in the interests of unlearning, growth, and change, should be the gradual formulation of a cognitive model of the world of education and the world of work to which he can bring a consistent set of values and attitudes. It is in this educational framework that the objectives of guidance and the objectives of teaching become inseparable in relation to the student.

It is imperative that the cognitive model developed by the student be a dynamic one if it is to serve him in his progress toward vocational maturity. Let us consider the major cognitive acquisitions that are relevant to the individual's vocational development, recognizing that they should provide the base upon which to structure a guidance information program. These constructs are:

1. That the future self is a combination of what the individual is, the ideal he holds, those whom he sees, and those from whom he learns.

2. That education is a process not only of maintaining the culture but of continuously creating a new and richer culture from all the inherent elements of our pluralistic society.

3. That the individual's personal concerns can be fulfilled through what he does; therefore, the focal point of vocational guidance should not be on the immediate availability of a choice of a particular vocation, but rather on the recognition of the need to plan the quality of one's future life.

These conceptual goals are not impractical philosophical ideals; practitioners would be remiss if they did not recognize their existence and attempt to make them factual realities through their day to day communication with students.

Many specific content elements, facts, and cause-effect relationships can be delineated within the purview of the above constructs, and a beginning effort to make these explicit and reduced to the practical will be set forth in later chapters.

In summary, we may conclude that in making a decision about the proper use of educational and vocational information in guidance we should consider it as part of a long-term developmental process. This process must place some emphasis on exploring motivational patterns prior to its concentration on vocational planning or decision-making. Over an extended period of time, a guidance program must use information in two ways: (1) to remove emotional obstacles that interfere with the individual's interaction with his environment and his rational processing of information and (2) to build cognitive structures (concepts, rules, principles) necessary to the individual's management of his own life. The author feels that using information in the above ways will not only motivate positive goal-seeking behavior but might aid in the prevention of frustration and emotional disruption with regard to achieving vocational goals.

## Whom Will the System Change and Why?

### Rationale for Change

Regardless of how noncommittal, ingenious, or objective we are inclined to be, we should recognize that we aid and abet a process of change in the student when we make use of the various sorts of available educational and vocational information. We must also realize that even if we were to do nothing, our "control" in the sense of impact on the life of the student would be no less influential and the consequences perhaps less desirable. Change is inherent — not only in the individual as a living organism, but in a society such as ours which is devoted to technological advance. Change is also inherent in the concept of career development with its various theoretical formulations that emphasize the state of "becoming" or "self-actualizing." Methods employed by counselors are practiced with the expectation that the change effected will be positive and satisfying to the needs of the student. It has been said that the counselor fears to intervene because he does not want to structure the student's goals, yet this very lack of intervention may initiate trends that become difficult to reverse at some later period in adult life.

### Whom and Why

In developing and communicating educational and vocational information, it is important to keep in mind the divergent motives and expectations of the kinds of students that we are attempting to reach. Much of the present educational and vocational information materials have been inordinately concerned with the college and professional bound and have been ineffective with less motivated and less academically talented youth. Although most counselors and teachers would agree that there are many variables that may influence an individual's motivation, there is still the tendency to label an individual "college" or "noncollege" at some point in his school progress. Let it be noted that there can be inherent danger in devising and using instruments and methods to make this labeling more precise. An even greater danger is that the label be given an emotionalized aura derived from the educator's value system rather than an acceptance of the need of society for abilities not developed in college. So in determining what interventions to make, the system designer or the dispenser of information should be careful not to put youth in a box.

If students are not to be labeled or categorized in terms of their post-high school careers, what should be the guidance specialist's perception of students? What mode of individual differences should be employed in order not to obscure the intentions and expectations of many individuals and groups? In attempting to answer some of these questions, the concern of educators seems to have focused on three groups: the *potential dropout,* the *affluent,* and the *female.*

### The Potential Dropout

The literature (Passow, 1963; Bruner, 1961; Frost and Hawkes, 1966) suggests that motivational patterns and values develop as a result of experiences and events that form the milieu to which an individual has been and continues to be exposed. It is important that practitioners understand the qualitatively different preparation for the learning process and the behavioral requirements of the school of children who have been exposed during their early years to an entirely different set of elements of our culture than those to which the practitioner may have been exposed. This has particular reference for the counselor in understanding the effect of experiential factors on the youth's perception of self.

Studies conducted at the University of Chicago (Short and Strodtbeck, 1968) with lower-class slum youth point up the fact that this particular group viewed themselves as "losers." Every time these youth examined the rational structure of our society and that of work in particular, they fit themselves into a place low in status. What these studies also report is that slum youth think that their failure to achieve is their own fault and that they are responsible for their low status. In other words, they believe in the rational consequence of rational action: "If I fail it is because I have been naughty; if I fail it is because I have not been good."

From the counseling and guidance point of view this means that even the "losers" can be reached in that they have the same set of motivations and aspirations as the rest of the youth in our society. Yet paradoxically, very few of these same youngsters believe they have the slightest chance of executing any plan they make. Here lies the incongruity: these youth assume the moral responsibility for failure but also have the belief that they cannot execute their plans. These results would appear to confirm the ascribed importance of "fate" as an intervening factor in realization of personal objectives and intentions that one finds among many members of this group.

So in terms of reaching and talking to this group, what is the system going to talk about? What message is it going to communicate? Even if these youth know what is to be done, their expectation of failure prevents them from doing it. Not only will they reject the information that the traditional guidance program provides, but they have difficulty in believing that the knowledge to be acquired from utilization of such data could possibly be applicable to them.

Present systems of information are mainly designed to deal with the problem of individual differences at the first surface level of cognitive learning and rote response. These findings all point to one thing — an information system that is to focus on human needs must recognize the psychological barriers that exist to a youth's vocational development.

When we examine the evidence on oral language ability and development of verbal skills, we find that deficiencies in these areas can be associated with stimulus, cultural, or experiential deprivation in early childhood years. A review of the literature reveals that ghetto children and those in disadvantaged areas are generally deprived of a number of aspects of middle class culture, such as education, reading material, and formal language (Riesman, 1962). Keller (1963) and Deutsch (1964) have noted that during the preschool years, children growing up in disadvantaged areas have had few objects to play with, particularly books, puzzles, pencils, or games. They have been exposed to a great deal of noise and confusion in their everyday life and have had limited opportunity to explore their immediate surroundings and neighborhood due to the unsafe conditions of their physical and social environment. In fact, most of their leisure time, not only in preschool but later growth years, is spent in relatively restricted and monotonous activities such as extended television watching or sleeping.

These studies conclude that lack of variety and order in the home and lack of sustained contact and interaction between children and parents often result in negative effects on language ability and the development of verbal skills. These negative effects apparently impede the development of such cognitive and verbal behaviors as labeling, relating, describing, interpreting, and communicating. Guidance activities aimed at personal growth and development generally require proficiency in communication and verbal interchange and the ability to organize, analyze, and interpret vocational information for personal planning and choice. Therefore, guidance materials and techniques must be developed that will give recognition to the deficiencies in cognitive skills of the type indicated above in order to move the individual from rudimentary *vocational awareness* to personal interpretation and *vocational planning*.

## The Affluent

Research findings accumulated from various studies of the affluent youngster (Scott & Voz, 1967; Miller, 1966; Tobias, 1969) indicate that students from middle and upper middle class or more socially and economically favored areas are more inclined to expect success and satisfaction in their future activities. This expectation appears to stem from confidence in their own abilities to meet the criteria of success. Conversely, some of these students tend to reach a frustration plateau in achievement motivation and reject the traditional criteria of success and satisfaction as not being meaningful in terms of their own lives when the expectation demands, both internal and external, become too intense. Ideally, they are seeking an environment which allows for autonomy, creativity, freedom to develop ideas, and individual achievement (self-realization).

Rosenthal (1969) has described this situation aptly:

> The problem faced by the middle classes and by white middle class youth in particular is not in the arbitrariness of events, but in the perceived tightness and inexorable quality of the causal systems in which they find themselves embedded. Whereas the black child soon learns that any false motion will toss him out of the roller-coaster, the middle class white child knows that he can safely perform some silly and taunting acrobatics without falling off his merry-go-round. His failures will not lead to his degradation but only to some less prestigious yet equally secure job.

An insight into an affective component of vocational behavior stemming from affluent youngsters' perception of themselves regarding the subject of job-seeking is provided by Martin (1967). Specifically it was found that the difficulties that students from more affluent homes expect in entering a vocational field lie more in the direction of getting the jobs they would like to have rather than in just getting jobs. The question of how to best resolve the decision process that comes about when they will be ready to enter the job market and start their first jobs seems foremost for this group. How are they to be sure that they are not getting *locked in* to something that is sterile and dead-end? How are they to be sure that they might not have a better opportunity tomorrow? These are pragmatic issues that create a great deal of anxiety when the youth in his affluent environment begins to consider how to make the best bargain he can for his future vocational life.

So we see that it is not only the so-called disadvantaged youth of the ghetto area and inner city who requires experience that will increase his sense of effectiveness but his suburban white cousin as well.

*The Female*

In spite of all the attention focused on federal, state, and local statistics relative to the rising percentages of women of all ages in the labor force, many counselors still approach the vocational counseling of girls from the perspective of the time-worn notion that for girls the idea of success is marriage and that a career is not important. This stems from the fact that too frequently in our society we are indoctrinated with the idea that work for the female is first and foremost a "man-hunting job," and that choice of a vocation even for intellectually gifted girls is relatively unimportant (Ohlsen, 1968). The modern girl today, like her male counterpart, is more and more inclined to seek to establish her own identity within or without marriage and the one means that society provides is through vocational pursuits. Despite this developing commonality of goal between the sexes, the information program in providing guidance must not neglect the fact that the female is biologically, psychologically, sociologically, educationally and anthropologically different than the male; hence she has different aspirations, values, and expectations regarding a satisfactory adult and work role. For this reason the counseling and guidance of girls must be approached in a different fashion from the counseling and guidance of boys in that they need special information.

On the one hand, young men in high school know that they must work. They also know that despite the fact that the older generation in the culture that controls them will adopt any expedient to delay their entry into the world of work, they will in due course fill or create the various work positions. Meanwhile, they can experiment; they can re-establish the masculine hairdo as a badge of virility and the beard as a sign of masculinity; and they can protest through the symbols of their music, their garb, and their special jargon as well as through their organized protest groups. But these young men know that they must eventually work and will probably do so all their lives.

On the other hand, girls know that they will not always work unless they have a great desire to do so and that their work life will be interrupted or curtailed (at least in the sense of being in the labor force) after marriage and particularly with the advent of children. The evolving pattern of the female's work life suggests that she will have three or perhaps four separate work careers rather than a lifetime of work. These developing patterns indicate that the future for the female will probably consist of a multilevel work life. These levels include:

(1) *The single girl.* The marriage age is steadily dropping and the sexual revolution and new methods of contraception provide today's young woman with a type of control over her fate formerly possessed only by males. The young woman's initial entry into the labor market provides her with money to escape parental control, establish her own apartment, buy the kind of clothes she wants, and "realize" or "fulfill" herself. It also provides the best place for her to meet young men and in due course her future husband.

(2) *Married and in economic straits.* In many cases there is an economic necessity for a wife to return to the world of work if the husband's income is limited or if some other personal or situational factor exists which requires such a move. Related circumstances would be where the couple feels the need for a higher standard of living and the comforts and conveniences which the extra salary would bring.

(3) *Married and with children.* Here we see the split-level work life for the woman in which she works prior to marriage, retires temporarily from the labor force while she bears her children, then returns to it again. The woman, fortunately, has special opportunities for part-time or seasonal work in many occupational fields and increasingly is able to establish her own conditions as to hours in vocational areas where there is high demand for particular skills.

(4) *Separated or divorced.* Girls today must realize the possibility that marriage may end in separation or divorce. The separated or divorced woman often finds that the support payments provided to her are insufficient for what she regards as the necessities for herself and her children. Thus she finds that a return to the work world will provide the additional income she requires. Moreover, the work site again becomes the best place to re-establish a network of masculine acquaintances and friendships.

(5) *Widowhood.* Statistics show that women on the average live longer than men. The young woman must recognize that she may face widowhood at about the time her own children are beginning to break the tie that links them to their homes and to their mothers. Again one of the most feasible solutions is work.

It would seem logical that if the woman is going to spend a great deal of her life in the labor force she needs to know early how she will spend these years. Even though she may have no intention in high school of using her training, she should initiate through her educational program some possible career-line for herself. If the female utilizes her foresight, she will not be left totally unprepared for entry into a vocational area if necessary or desirous in later years. These are important considerations that girls should keep in mind as they make educational and vocational choices and plan their lives.

Another reason the female needs special information and guidance while still in school is that she has an advice-giving function that the male of the species does not have. First, it is the girl friend that the young man turns to during periods of self-discovery and identity-seeking as the only person he can trust to listen to him and respect his self-doubts and fears. She must be able to listen and relate one fact to another and also relate these facts to what she knows about the world to assist him in these troubled times. Second, in rearing her children, the female, now mother, must be prepared to induct her children into the culture and the world of work. She must be prepared to teach them the nature of work; what it means to have discipline (how to plan and complete a task), what it means to profess a vocational area (to openly affirm faith in the truth and goodness of what one is doing), and finally, what it means not to be upset by the inconveniences and petty details of the pressures and requirements of work.

Hence it is apparent that there is a difference in counseling boys and counseling girls. Inherent in the boy's vocational life is a single-minded purpose; therefore his vocational plans can be mapped out more readily than those of his female counterpart. This does not mean that he will not encounter extended periods of trial and error, either by accident or choice, but eventually he will find a niche. Girls need more systematic help in learning to deal with a man-made world and in finding their way in this world in terms of themselves, their children, and the men who are or will be important in their lives.

In summary, we may conclude that individual differences and subpopulations are important variables to be considered in reaching individuals with educational and vocational information. For this reason it is necessary to determine the extent to which the guidance materials being developed are generally sensitive to the vocational problems of the individuals and groups with whom they will be used. Recognizing the nature of today's student, the changing social consciousness, and today's employment milieu will be an integral part of preparing vocational guidance materials and information processing systems for a new generation.

## How Will the Change be Effected?

The introduction of new equipment media in education (computers, television, audiovisual and other communications media) and the impact of behavioral research on curriculum planning and teaching-learning methodology has influenced not only the design of instructional programs but the development of new technologies for counseling and guidance. These approaches or systems fall into two groups: (1) the development of information retrieval and computer-based training systems and (2) the development of multimedia interactive learning systems. The theoretical and methodological considerations on which these approaches are based are often quite dissimilar.

### Information Retrieval and Computer-Based Training Models

An analysis of the design of existing computer-based and other mechanized systems for vocational information processing as reported by Perrone and Thrush (1969) reveals that these approaches tend to cluster along a continuum that could be characterized at one end by systems corresponding to information retrieval systems (e.g., Project

VIEW, Project VISION, Project VOGUE, The Rochester Career Guidance Project), and at the other end by systems corresponding to vocational decision training systems (e.g., The Information System for Vocational Decision [ISVD], Computerized Vocational Information Systems [CVIS] and the Total Guidance Information Support System [TGISS]). Both positions have something to contribute to the provision of information for guidance in effecting change.

The data banks of occupational information for those systems characterized primarily as *retrieval systems* utilize the type of material provided by the U.S. Department of Labor, and their emphasis is upon such devices as the *Dictionary of Occupational Titles* (DOT) for the communication of relevant information on jobs and work. The objectives for these systems are generally twofold: (1) the task of cataloging the types of available jobs (local, regional, or national) to identify the full array of existing and emerging job opportunities and their relevant worker traits and skills; and (2) the task of relating this information to a personalized data profile on the student in order to make available to the student appropriate occupational information stored in the system. Some systems have compiled data banks for the retrieval of information on education and personal and family living, as well as on occupations and work.

Probability measurement techniques are used to relate the personal data on the student to pertinent data about education, family, training and/or work. The assumption that is implicit when supplying this type of information is that the student is capable of assimilating and absorbing such information and exercising some rational choice in a complex analysis of the problem of educational and vocational choice making.

The computer-based systems characterized as *training systems* have as their primary purpose the design of a process to more actively engage the individual in the choice process.

In brief, data banks of information similar to those described above are compiled for computer processing and retrieval purposes. In addition, the computer is assigned an important monitoring or supervisory function to insure that the student's interactive experience with the information in the system is fitted to the prediction of what it is the system thinks he now needs to know. Ideally, the monitoring function should be programmed to detect what the student does with the information supplied and then provide feedback information to the student to enable him to discover how he has been using the information and the utility that it has had for him. The ultimate goal of the training system is that the individual become self-correcting and gradually acquire some comprehension of his decision-making development as he proceeds with his use of the system. Thus, the challenge to computer-based training systems is to program for self-learning and the mutual accommodation of the individual and the system over time (Tiedemann, 1968, 1969). This goal has yet to be realized.

### Learning Models and Interactive Media for Effecting Change

Super's theory of self-concept has had considerable influence on research and practice in vocational development (1951, 1963). In self-concept theory, the starting point must always be the individual's own knowledge and self-perceptions, however distorted or limited they may be, concerning self and the process of occupational choice. Self-concept theory thus includes motivational and personality variables which may influence the self-perceptions of the youngster and cause him to adopt a different appraisal of himself than that made by others. An explanation of the ways in which socio-economic status influences the types of occupations that an individual feels are appropriate for him is also provided by this theory.

Despite the attention directed by Super and other theorists to motivational and sociological variables and their relationship to vocational development, guidance information practice seems scarcely touched by these theoretical insights. In fact, media information materials have seldom been produced and made operational from the theoretical base of the complementary relationship of the developing self-concept and occupational information.

Evidence presented earlier in this monograph indicates that many youngsters are seldom ready for the type of information processing that *retrieval* and *training* systems require. The assumption implicit when these types of experiences are provided to the student is that the individual's motivational patterns are set and known and that he is now ready for the cognitive process of decision-making. It appears obvious that for the larger proportion of students, a great deal of prerequisite emotional and conceptual growth and development must take place prior to their applying particular types of cognitive responses to the information provided.

Let us look at some significant media and methods for effecting cognitive and affective change that are undergoing development for use in counseling and guidance and consider when and how these techniques might be employed.

#### Behavioral Counseling

Krumboltz (1966) has been foremost in proposing the usefulness of reinforcement theory and behavioral counseling as a model for the counseling and guidance field. His research activities have focused on the investigation of the use of reinforcement techniques in changing the personal behavior of individuals. These techniques, when put into practice, utilize operant conditioning models as a means of developing all types of learning (Skinner, 1953). In behavioral counseling, "motivation" is externally contrived through deprivation and reward, and "purpose" is created through arbitrary determination of what behaviors to reinforce and what behaviors not to reinforce to achieve some terminal behavior set by the "conditioner." Thus, reward in this system remains *extrinsic* and is something that is under the control of those who manipulate the system.

Directly related to these basic research concerns are applied studies conducted by Krumboltz and his colleagues of vocational problem-solving experiences and their impact on student behavior. Pertinent to these studies are materials and techniques designed to teach the student the actual process of problem-solving and decision-making (Gelatt, 1962; Yabroff, 1964), or provide prescriptive guidance and prescribed learning experiences (PLE's) for problem correction or remediation in aiding the student to successfully complete the sequence of developmental tasks determined desirable for the student (Jones, 1970). The design of these guidance objectives and materials has been greatly influenced by the theoretical concerns of Krumboltz in reinforcement and behavioral counseling.

Elementary school counseling programs that view the counselor as a consultant in analyzing the problems, academic or behavioral, of the student are beginning to advocate reinforcement therapy for behavioral change. In this case, the counselor and teacher individualize for each child what objective behaviors are desirable and what reinforcers would be most rewarding in developing these behaviors. The behaviors selected and the strategies employed may be as simple as setting up reinforcement contingencies to keep the child in his seat or to differentially reinforce the child's discrimination of the symbols $p$ and $q$ and $d$ and $b$.

A great part of the success of the reinforcement approach depends upon a very careful structuring of the reward system and the ability of the counselor and teacher to be constantly alert and flexible in developing new means of reinforcement. The assumption is that once the behavior has been acquired and maintained, one can eliminate extrinsic reward to a considerable extent and that intrinsic reward somehow begins to take over. This appears to be an erroneous assumption, however. Extrinsic reward and externally contrived motivation may provide movement in a prescribed direction but the types of human learning resulting from these controls are qualitatively different than the types of human learning resulting from the introduction of intrinsic forms of reward and motivation. Also, there is no reason to believe and quite a few reasons to doubt that conditioning and behavioral modification are the antecedent conditions for motivation and purposive behavior.

For the purposes of behavioral counseling and vocational development, if we really wish to deal with the variables of intrinsic reward and motivation, the best procedure would be to deal with them directly.

## Humanistic Guidance

Jenkins (1969) has noted that although for many years a relationship between cognitive information learning and affective acceptance has been assumed to exist, recent research raises serious questions about the tenability of this assumption. Krathwohl and others (1956) report, "The evidence suggests that affective behaviors develop when appropriate learning experiences are provided for students much the same as cognitive behaviors develop from appropriate learning experiences." This implies, certainly, that an acquisition in one domain may not necessarily result in a similar attainment in the other. In fact, Krathwohl further reports that "under some conditions the development of cognitive behaviors may actually destroy certain desired affective behaviors." The analogue of this would be that the development of certain affective behaviors may actually destroy certain desired cognitive behaviors. These findings pose certain problems for choice of media and methodology in effecting change as part of the new curriculum concern being voiced by educators today (Martin, 1969a).

Let us take for the moment a pragmatic point of view. The question arises as to how we might in the course of achieving certain guidance objectives and goals provide experiences which intrinsically satisfy both the affective and cognitive needs of the youngster. Therapeutic experiences such as role play, doll play, self-help groups, etc., operate on the principle that an experience is intrinsically rewarding if it is structured in such a way as to allow the individual involved to derive personal meaning from the experience in terms of his own anxieties and concerns. How can we capitalize on this principle in the development of an interactive system of guidance between practitioner and child that will focus on a broader reality than that proposed by behavioristic developments — meaning that in making the system operational it must consider the person not as an object but must consider how the person and perspective of the observer and the person and perspective of the observed affect the meaningfulness of the communication that takes place between them (Rogers, 1964; Combs and Snygg, 1959).

*Humanistic guidance,* as defined by the author, denotes a broader scope of variables to be considered in the design of a guidance information system than has heretofore been considered. These variables include perceptual responses such as intentions and expectations, values, purposes and goals. To accomplish its objectives the humanistic system would tend to place behavior modification strategies in a broader phenomenological context. The methodological questions to be raised in employing this approach are, first, how can we organize guidance information for human processing so that it describes and represents the psycho-social aspects of the world; and second, how can we communicate these psycho-social aspects so that the individual experiences these elements in a manner similar to the manner in which he experiences them in the real world. The value of developing a method of organizing and communicating information in guidance in this manner and form is obvious. First, it will provide a means for involving the individual at the affective level and for encouraging him to respond with the way he feels, or the "truth" as he sees it (an important objective as stated earlier). Second, it will provide a means for establishing the conditions under which the individual can learn to recognize and articulate the separate elements of the information he is experiencing, and interrelate and interpret these personal experiences within a larger framework or whole — the larger framework being the structure or model on which the psycho-social elements are based.

In humanistic guidance, reward is intrinsic to the system and operates through the process of reduction of anxiety as the individual is exposed to a given sequence of learning experiences. In this case, anxiety reduction is related to the amount of uncertainty that is reduced for the individual as he discovers and attaches personal meaning to events in the real world through the dynamics of the above proposed process.

Seldom has audio-visual media been used for humanistic vocational guidance through the use of elements of image and sound although such media has great potential for providing content and technique for simulating and modeling adjustive experience. Directly related to these concerns Martin (1969b) after considerable research has developed situational films based on psycho-social models and themes drawn from theoretical and empirical vocational guidance research. The use of visual imagery and sound provides relevant realistic stimuli which, due to their open-ended nature, create an environment for affective response. The dynamic interaction in the group discussion which follows each presentation is instrumental in motivating growth and change at the affective level. Audiorecording of individual responses provides an important phenomenological device for the student and the practitioner.

The dynamic interaction that occurs in the student group may be expressed in various types of responses. Some students may express slight hostility, resistance, or resentment; some may use analytic comparison; some may merely make observations; some may have positive feelings; some may have negative feelings. But, as these responses are evoked and expressed during the interaction, the students are able to identify and clarify for themselves concepts and feelings involved in their statements of vocational expectations and plans.

The media in this case is used as a tool to stimulate awareness aspects of the viewer related to concepts and expectations of self, education, work, family, and community. The technique has been so designed as *not* to place the individual in a totally ambiguous, anxiety-producing situation as do many "sensitivity" methods. In brief, the media not only motivates the individual to respond but its structured affective nature provides support during the dynamics of group interaction while the individual is imposing his own meaning and interpretation on the open-ended behavioral sequences he has viewed in the stimulating elements of image and sound.

The experience can be intrinsically satisfying to the youngster, particularly as he begins to see the larger whole of the total experience to which he has been and is being exposed and of which any of the individual experiences is only a part. It is hypothesized that *intrinsic* reward will be a much more powerful reinforcer than *extrinsic* reward — intrinsic reward being related to the reduction in anxiety prerequisite to the unlearning of affective responses.

In summary, in reviewing the various media and methodology for effecting change, we could conclude that the student and the practitioner, where possible, should be provided with an opportunity in a humanistic guidance framework to learn to analyze and interpret data in terms of intrinsic values and concepts of what is meaningful to the student. The assumption is that the learner does have the right to know what is happening to him and that guidance should be more than a matter of the individual responding to external rewards and punishments that condition his behavior. If this is true, the system should provide the student a way of learning about the forces which act upon his choices and decisions. Guidance information systems under development also need to consider strategies that will provide the use of social models which give relevance to what he is learning as well as intrinsic reward.

In the preceding chapter it was noted that the major objective of the new goals of education is the design of a total instructional program that is responsive to the predicament of the individual in today's school and society. Therefore, a guidance information system should strive to serve the individual in his humanness, at his point in his functioning. It should recognize that the means that it will use will affect the ends that it expects to achieve. It should embrace the concept that the individual must learn to know and appraise what is happening to him and its relevance to what he believes and intends in his developmental process of career choice. Humanistic guidance confirms the involvement of the total human being in decision-making.

# 3

# An Information-Learning Model for Guidance[1]

## The Need

A review of the development and dissemination of career information discussed at a conference held at the University of Pittsburgh in March, 1966 (Martin, 1966), indicated that little attention had been focused on the various ways in which occupational information should be communicated and that the education-learning aspect of career development had scarcely been explored. Guidance programs, in general, consist of a fragmented stab at "career days," occupational brochures, and traditional job descriptions. Educational and vocational information, as traditionally presented, is still primarily limited to the printed page with the occasional use of films or film strips. The larger proportion of such materials lack sensitivity to the problems of youth in a complex technological society. In addition, these materials and the procedures for their use generally reflect little sensitivity to the ethnic and social characteristics of the larger proportion of our school population and to the vocational problems of special subpopulations

[1] An earlier draft of this model was submitted as part of a final report to the office of Education, U.S. Department of Health, Education and Welfare, Contract No. OE 6–85–052, Jan., 1968.

such as the potential dropout or the female. Further, guidance information is most often developed as an aid to the guidance counselor or teacher rather than oriented toward the individual student.

The question of how to develop new types of much needed career information (particularly for black and disadvantaged youth) and how to integrate this information into the school curriculum requires careful consideration and thorough investigation.

It seems that the problem of *how* to communicate occupational information is as little understood as *what* to communicate. It is time, however, that educators re-evaluate the prevailing assumptions as to what kinds of occupational information are appropriate for career development and for what sub-populations, what media may best be utilized, and how career information should be integrated into the curriculum.

How can career information be organized as part of the formal curriculum and be communicated to all students to increase effectively their career-planning skills? The importance of this question to the students, to the parents, to the schools, and to the nation is obvious since one of the major reasons for a youth's failure to cope with the adult environment is his inability to get and keep a job or derive satisfaction from his work.

Obviously, comprehensive research and development efforts should be undertaken to design a comprehensive system of guidance information media and methodology for its use for the vocational guidance of all youth. Such a system would be set in a developmental framework and would be implemented as part of the formal educational process.

## The Model

The information-learning model for guidance relates to a method of stimulating and motivating students to be knowledgeable about such aspects as themselves and their role and the role of education and training them to achieve a beneficial adult and work life. Today's youth, while at the student level, require knowledge of and specific motivation toward goals that will permit them in their later adult life to participate constructively and with dignity in our community life, hence, which will enable them to achieve for themselves personal satisfaction and accomplishment. As discussed in Chapter 2, the need for motivation at the student level is of particular importance to the disadvantaged youth who in many instances does not receive this motivation and knowledge in his conventional day-to-day home life and general environment. The disadvantaged youth of today needs information and learning experiences that will enable him to develop more effective planning and problem solving skills for realizing his intentions and goals.

In brief, the primary objective of this information model is to introduce a formal method of motivational and humanistic guidance for all youth. The model takes into account the relationship between affective and cognitive learning in effecting change.

The design of the model is based on the following assumptions:

1. That communications designed from elements of image and sound can be articulated and modeled to present psycho-social aspects of the environment that normally could only be referred to obliquely and tangentially (by the guidance specialist) in an oral presentation or through print.

2. That communications of this nature and format will broaden the range of stimuli to which the individual will respond, hence, broaden awareness on the part of the individual to the psychological and social aspects of human behavior projected by the stimulating elements of the media.

3. That a method for individual motivation that embodies stimulating elements based on valid psycho-social models and schemes and a technique for communicating them will enable each individual to relate the information to his existing personal knowledge and experiences for the purpose of establishing realistic and practical actions and goals.

4. That stimulus events as described above, when reinforced by the individual comparing his responses to the responses of other individuals similarly stimulated, will result in a reduction in the intensity of affect and increase the willingness of the individual to engage in a variety of career development activities that previously had little intrinsic value for him.

## The Information Component

The selected stimulus elements, for the purpose of motivation to achieve a beneficial work life, are directed to stimulate the interrelated informational aspects of *self, education,* and *work* at the generic, specific, and interrelated levels.

### Generic Level

At the generic level the function that information should perform is to aid the student in formulating vocational concepts and ideas. *Self,* at the generic level, encompasses the wide range of specific differences to be found among students. *Self* is to be defined as more than the limited concept of interests and abilities but is to be expanded to include values, expectations, psychological needs, biases, perceptions, and response sets as they form the backdrop for the individual's experiential background. *Education,* at the generic level, refers to the wide variety, complexity, and range of forms of learning available to students in all intellectual and economic levels of our society. *Education* is to be defined in terms of its usefulness as a tool to enable the student to create a full life for himself and achieve self-actualization in the world of work. *Work,* at the generic level, refers to the scope and range of activities required of workers by the many types of jobs available in today's society. In general, the goal at the generic level is to communicate and stimulate the student in the aspects of awareness of the scope and variety of technological functions that currently exist and to provide the student with the motivation to explore these domains of function in relation to his own experiences and recognized and actual goals.

### Specific Level

The function that information should perform at the specific level is to provide facts for the student in regard to his personal, psychosocial, and educational differences as individual or group need for specific information arises. The information aspect at this level is intended to motivate the student toward a realization of his specific attributes in relation to the general existing attributes of students so that in effect he may categorize himself specifically in relation to individuals generally. *Education,* at the specific level, denotes characteristics of educational institutions specifically including their values and aspirations and the range of corresponding values, aspirations, educational and vocational capabilities, and skills that are achieved through the way such institutions are organized. *Work,* at the specific level, refers to the characteristics of a job-worker situation and the required performance characteristics of given specific jobs. The goal at this level is to have the three aspects of *self, education,* and *work* take on more specific meaning for the individual and to motivate and enable him to relate the appropriateness and feasibility of his particular qualifications, attributes, personal and social characteristics, education and training to specific educational and vocational intentions and desires.

### Interrelated Level

The function that information is to perform at the interrelated level is the development of individual inquiry and problem-solving skills. At this level, the student is motivated to obtain and apply his knowledge of job data, his education and training, and his awareness of patterns of behavior as they would interact in a particular environment. The goal at this level is to insure that the complex interrelationship of specific factors, including personal, social, economic, and educational, provides an appropriate and realistic motivational basis to enable the individual to apply his concepts and knowledge regarding work-life selection in planning and decision-making and to determine for himself appropriate action to achieve his intended adult and work-life goals.

Thus, what is to be taught is structure and methodology, including key concepts, basic generalizations, and knowledge for dealing with practical situations and problems of choice. The content of the guidance information becomes a means which influences the ends — a resource rather than an end in itself.

### The Behavioral Component

A behavioral component on which the design of information input described above can be based is described here:

A basic postulate guiding the development of the behavioral inputs is that man as a system is primarily active, which presupposes that his learned behavior leads to more complex forms of organizations and integration as part of the developmental learning process; if he were primarily a reactive system it would lead to more singular forms of acquisition and extinction as part of the conditioning process. Therefore, inherent in the learning structure of the guidance curriculum to be evolved are the assumptions: (1) that there is a hierarchy of development leading from the rudimentary behavior of "experiencing" to the more complex behavior of rational "planning"; (2) that cognitive and affective behavior has coordinate significance and is intertwined; (3) that purpose is intrinsic to that which is to be learned; (4) that responses are not single but multiple and are made simultaneously to more than one factor in the learning situation; and (5) that transfer is based on emphasizing generalizability rather than similarity of situations to probable use of what is to be learned.

Therefore, guidance as an implementing factor in the learning and development process must be primarily concerned with the individual's vocational stage of development which would include his ability to process certain kinds of information, his motivation to form new concepts, and his skill in applying his own knowledge for specific purposes.

The basic dimensions of this component can be viewed from two general domains of learning, the cognitive and the affective (see Figure 1). The cognitive domain includes a general multiplicity of types of learning: (1) verbal chaining, (2) concept formation, (3) problem solving.[2] The affective domain consists of other types of learning: (1) awareness, (2) valuing, (3) organization of a value

---

[2] Experimental evidence for eight basic types of learning has been provided recently by Robert M. Gagne in *The Conditions of Learning* (New York: Holt, Rinehart and Winston, Inc., 1965).

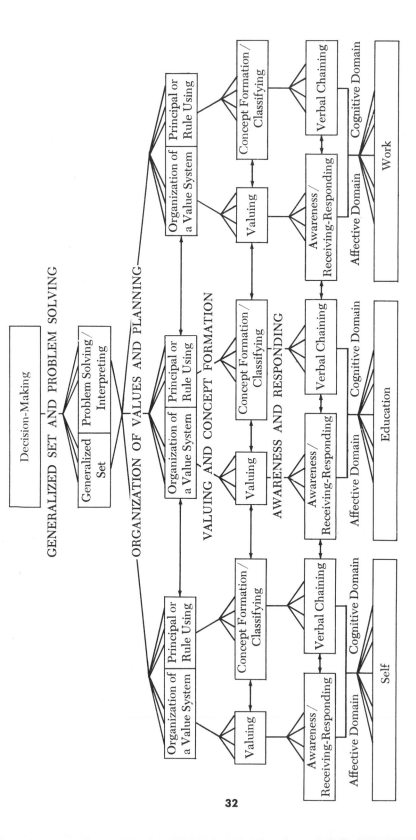

**FIGURE 1**
**A behavioral model for the development of media**

32

system.[3] The interrelations among the many behavioral outcomes of the various types of learning form a complex system of interactions and types of response that need to be taken into account in learning experiences for vocational planning and goal-setting.

### The Media Component

The multimedia component of the Information-Learning Model is formulated on the assumption that environments for various types of learning must be considered consistent with what we know about the effectiveness of various communications media (e.g., film, stills, audiotape, programmed instruction) used in combination with a variety of modes of instruction (e.g., lecture, discussion, recitation, laboratory exercise). For example, one might hypothesize that to broaden awareness of self, education, and work (i.e., to increase the range of vocational development stimuli to which the individual will now respond), the audio-visual stimulus reinforced by group discussion could impart to the student a heightened degree of self, of the possibility of self-enhancing educational attainment, and awareness of potential work he can do. It is to be noted that the dynamics of "discussion" as a learning experience becomes a medium in itself through which the concepts presented by the stimulus material are reinforced and the attributes of the concepts discussed are broadened and made meaningful to the individual student.

Within this complex framework, media can be designed on the basis of the information inputs which must be communicated in connection with the types of learning to be acquired. For example, media designed for the cognitive domain may include the communication of those informational inputs that deal with the application skills of vocational problem-solving and decision-making. In the affective domain, media may consider the communication of those informational inputs that deal with the acquisition skills of awareness and valuing.

With an indication of the terminal behavioral outcomes in mind, multimedia measures based on behavioral elements suggested in the conceptual model can be tested to evaluate the differential impact of the several types of materials used under varying conditions. Stated differently, a given class of media could then be tested against the theoretical considerations of the model thus allowing predictions to be made as to certain specified behavioral changes (cognitive and affective) in students as a result of their interactions with such media.

---

[3] No systematic summary of the experimental evidence for types of affective behaviors is available. D. Krathwohl, B. Bloom, and B. Masia provide some clarity to affective domain terminology in their recent handbook, *Taxonomy of Educational Goals, Handbook II: Affective Domain* (New York: David McKay Company, Inc., 1964).

## Summary

In summary, educational outcomes of guidance may be evaluated in terms of students' awareness of values, aspirations, and expectations with respect to self, education, and work or their knowledge and problem-solving skill in applying information relative to self, education, and work in their own vocational planning and choice as a result of their exposure to a developmental guidance sequence of materials and activities.

Based on the above rationale, the design and use of guidance curriculum media as part of a comprehensive program of guidance can be outlined and delineated. The system's design should make explicit a process whereby the student would be guided to understand his affective behavior and then build cognitive skills for vocational planning and goal-setting. An initial attempt to set forth a developmental guidance curriculum based on the above rationale is set forth in Chapter 5. First, however, let us consider ways in which the guidance practitioner might learn more about the youth he is to serve before we consider the general aspects of a guidance curriculum designed for the needs of youth.

# 4

# Identifying Information Needs

The central thesis of this monograph has been that educational and vocational information does make a difference for the crucial problem of life adjustment of the youth, including that of occupational choice. It points out that the practitioner (guidance counselor, teacher, librarian) must work out a better way of providing the youngster with a great deal more information about educational programs and jobs than the youth is able to find without their help. Implicit in its pages is the belief that it is not to be expected that the child or youth will fulfill himself as an adult simply on the basis of his being loved and given secure support and protection, or seeing that the Oedipus complex is satisfactorily resolved, although these events should not be discounted as unimportant. The critical questions raised by this monograph are what kinds of information, knowledge, and wisdom should a guidance practitioner have concerning education, jobs and work and how is this information to be accumulated and utilized for the counseling of youth.

When one attempts to obtain a consensus as to what the guidance practitioner ought to have in the way of information on education and work, the message one invariably gets back is that practitioners need to know more about the child and need to obtain a better understanding of his attributes and motivational dispositions. The consensus appears to be this: That counseling and guidance practice does not entail providing general information on occupations and careers. That information in general is provided by such volumes as for example the

*Occupational Outlook Handbook* or the *Chronicle Guidance Series;* but, as we well know, this type of general information often goes over the heads of the individual students.

In practice this means that guidance personnel must learn more about youth than they have permitted themselves to learn so far. The guidance function in the American schools instills in its personnel the need to act as though they know all the answers as to what is right and what is real for students in the particular community that their school serves — and quite often this simply isn't true. This is particularly the case with reference to low income people, girls, blacks, and other minority groups. Put another way, it is important that the school counselor try to get a better "fix" on students as humans. The counselor must learn better how to reach the individual youngster where he is, to serve him in his humanness, and to find means of aiding the youngster in achieving an understanding of and practical approach to the management of his own life.

To do this, the guidance practitioner should seek opportunities to look at the problems of youngsters through their own eyes and in their own terms. It is only in this way that he can begin to understand the kinds of demands that the institutions of the family, school and community are placing on the youngster and the kinds of pressures that youngsters are exposed to in the processes of making choices.

Based on the assumption that counselors first need to know more about the youngsters they are serving, the counseling interview can become a significant means for acquiring first hand information and data on what individual students need to know. To obtain this information most effectively, the counselor should carefully construct interviewing situations in the course of which the youngster can candidly discuss himself, his relations with others, and the problems with which he has to cope. (Group discussion sessions could also be developed as a vehicle for this purpose.) If the counselor is not only skillful in his use of the interviewing (or group discussion) technique but also perceptive when listening to what is said, then he should be able to see (hopefully with a minimum of distortion) such things as how the youngsters see school, how they see their families, what things they would like to do, what things they fear doing, what their aspirations and expectations are, and what their feelings are with respect to education and work. Information and data of this kind, when properly interpreted, will not only aid the practitioner in determining the information needs of the student, but can also be used by the practitioner to aid him in his attempt to effect decent educational change for the youngster involved — change that will enable the youngster to take positive steps in the direction of his major goals.

To illustrate the manner in which the counseling interview may be developed as a useful strategy for determining information needs, examples will be provided. The following are excerpts from a series of interviews conducted with two students over a period of time.[4] Both of these students are black. Case examples of black students were chosen since they provide insights into the motivational dispositions of a minority group that we know little about. The first example typifies the kind of black youngster whom the school has identified as a potential dropout. The second example typifies the kind of black youngster that the school has identified as having the wherewithal to make it.

The interview excerpts reveal confusions on the part of the two students with respect to accurate knowledge of educational programs and work opportunities and options and alternatives perceived. Problems of conflicting roles are also revealed. Implications for the individual information needs are then delineated.

### Example I

The first excerpts are from interview sessions with a 15-year-old high school student identified as a potential dropout. The counselee comes from a family of fourteen children and is in the tenth grade. He had to repeat the seventh grade.

#### Accuracy of What School Has to Offer and Motives for Going There

The "choice" of the high school the counselee will attend was fairly passive, due primarily to the influence of a coach-teacher, Mr. S., which the counselee acknowledges:

I: What other sports are you involved with?
R: Football. I don't play with no teams. I'm going to R. high school to play for their football team, *that where Mr. S. is sending me.*
I: How did it come up?
R: He said I looked like a football player, and then he asked me did I play football. I said yes. So he said the best place for you to go is R. high school 'cause he's going to teach, he's going to be the coach of football over there. He said if I do good at football and basketball like I did in junior high, I'll get scholarships at college. So he came over to my house, and then he talked it over with my father and everything. That's why I'm going there, scholarships.

[4] This material was taken from interview material researched and compiled for the author by Diana Dolgoff, Pathways Project, Graduate School of Education, Harvard University. Miss Dolgoff was assisted by Robert A. Rosenthal and Bernard Bruce, Co-Directors of the Project. The material was assembled to be used in the course of the author's own efforts in the design of guidance information materials.

I: And you said you want to go to R. High School. Why do you want to go there?

R: For one thing, they got a lousy football team, and I want to go over there and play football to try to make it better, their football team better 'cause I can play football pretty good.

---

I: Well, how are your friends doing in school?

R: Well, most of them, they do pretty good work, but they like to joke around a lot.

I: Say, Richard, how is he doing? How are his grades?

R: All his grades are good, he ain't failed any subjects yet, but I think this marking period he might fail science cause he jokes around in science a lot.

I: Does he like school?

R: Yes, he likes school. He wants to go to college when he finishes.

I: How far do you think he will go in school?

R: I think he will go through college, keep going.

I: Has he ever talked to you about dropping out?

R: No.

I: Well, when he's out of school what kind of work do you think he will do?

R: *I don't know, he never talks about what he's going to do later when he comes back from college, he never talks about it.*

I: How is George doing in school?

R: He says he's going to have to go to summer school cause he's flunking Algebra and everything. Well, he goes to Tech. I don't know much about him.

I: Does he like school?

R: He doesn't like it too much, but he said he was going to go on through high school and after he finishes the twelfth he's going to drop out.

I: Well, how far do you think he will go?

R: I think he'll go to the tenth myself. See, he likes to fool around, he says he's tired of school, so I don't know, but I think he'll go to the tenth grade, then he'll quit.

I: Well, have you talked to him about dropping out?

R: No, not too much. He might say 'I think I'll drop out of school' and then we'll start laughing and say 'do you want to be a dummy or something?' We'll say 'you better stay in school.'

I: Have you ever talked about what kind of work he will do when he gets out of school?

R: No.

I: Well, what do you think he will be like when he's twenty-five?

R: He'll be a heavy-set man, I know that. He's going to go out for high school basketball. I don't think he'll play 'cause he's too big, for his size he's kind of fast, but when he gets around twenty-five he'll be too heavy, I guess, slow him up.

This section brings up a couple of themes which are central to the way that the counselee perceives the school situation. There is nothing waiting at the end of all this training . . . in fact it is not perceived as training at all, but almost as an obedience-intelligence center to which all young human animals are sent. The more they stay in, the less likelihood they will become stupid. But they will not be *more* anything, except "maybe a little smarter." Nor will they be prepared for anything. George, at age twenty-five, is described by the counselee only in terms of what he is now . . . playing basketball and heavy set.

What is suggested here in the way of information input is the need for models. The counselee knows that school is the avenue to success, and that sports is the avenue to success . *within* school, at least for George and himself. But he doesn't know what success is in any terms other than those of school . . . because he has no models of what successful educated people *do* (other than that they are "smart").

### Relationship of the School Experience to Pursuit of Occupational Goals

The next interview was concerned with skills required for a job and where training can be received: The counselee has a fairly good idea of the range of things he'll have to know to succeed as a mechanic or as a plumber, his occupational choices at this time (his father works as a tire man in a garage and he has seen a plumber at work). He thinks that college is necessary to realize both of these choices.

I: What do you have to do to become a mechanic?
R: Some people say you gotta go to college. Some say you've got to watch them and ask them what you got to do and everything.
I: Where would you go to school for this kind of training?
R: What school? I'd go to college.
I: Are you thinking of the military service as a possibility for training?
R: The Army or something? Yes, Yes, the mechanics train in the Army. To fix the cars up. You learn a little bit there.
I: What do you have to do to become a plumber?
R: Go to college.
I: Would the Army be a possibility for training?
R: I don't know.
I: What kind of training do you think you'd need to become a plumber?
R: Watch plumbers work.
I: Where do you think you'd go to school for this? You mentioned college. Do you have an idea which one?
R: No.

---

135114

R: Yes, he (father) agrees that I should go to college, but I don't feel the same about that part.

I: What's your feeling about that?

R: Going to college? I think that when I come out of the twelfth grade, I'll be smart enough to do a good job.

These two dialogues lead one to believe that the counselee has two conceptions of college. The first sounds like an apprenticeship program or "on the job training" which he calls college. Perhaps it is less a set of two different conceptions of college . . . perhaps college signifies any sort of advanced training beyond the high school stage. One sort (the apprenticeship-type) will qualify him to be a mechanic or a plumber. The other type (which is connected in his mind with football scholarships, a college course in high school, good grades, money, and being accepted at the school) — this type of college is that which is necessary to have a "good" job, like "sitting behind a desk." The next excerpt points up this difference.

I: What does your father want you to be?

R: He says he don't mind, just as long as I'm not a mechanic. Sitting behind a desk.

I: What does he like about sitting-behind-a-desk jobs?

R: He says instead of working, you're really sitting behind a desk telling other people what to do. *Wants me to go to college, get a better job. Wind up sitting behind a desk.*

It is evident from this perception that the counselee has that desk jobs and mechanic jobs require different types of college although he is not sure what college is. It is also evident that plumbing and auto mechanics are the only jobs that are real to this student and this knowledge has not come through the school but has come through personal contact and personal communication. Perhaps because he doesn't know other jobs, he cannot relate what he is learning now to what he will be doing as an adult if he does finish school.

### The Counselee's Perception of School

I: We've talked to a lot of high school and junior high school boys. Now, some say school is okay, and others think it's a drag, and the whole system is for the birds. How do you feel about school?

R: I think school is all right. If it weren't for school a lot of these people would be out being tramps and everything. But they went to school to learn a little bit, and know what to do with their money.

So far we see that the counselee is thoroughly imbued with the idea that the school is an important and worthy institution, although he might not like it or understand it. In fact, he displays little enthusiasm for his experiences in it. School makes people "smart," they can hold good jobs, be sensible about their money, and not be tramps. However, what the content of their intelligence will be and what specific use to which it can be put is almost completely blank in his mind.

 I: What do the teachers think of the kids?
 R: What do they think of the kids? Pests.
 I: And what do you think of what the kids think of the teacher?
 R: Kill them or something.
 I: Have you seen things that you would like to do, but haven't done, at Junior High?
 R: No. Yeah, once in a while I would like to beat up a couple of teachers. But I don't do it.

Not only is school incomprehensible, puzzling or meaningless, all the while a necessity, but it is also hostile, and frustrating. It is something for which one is always on guard.

 I: Is there any difference in Negro teachers and white teachers in how they treat the kids or how they teach?
 R: Well, the Negro teachers, they're strict. The white ones, they don't do nothing.
 I: If you could be taught by mainly Negro teachers or mainly white teachers, which would you pick?
 R: I would pick the Negro.
 I: Why?
 R: Because they're very strict. They won't let you slide . . . and if . . . the whitie let you do what you want, you don't learn nothing. But with the Negro teacher, you learn something.

---

 I: If you have a choice, would you rather be taught by men teachers or by women teachers?
 R: Men teachers.
 I: Why is that?
 R: Like I said, they're strict. Either learn, or get out. Just kick you out of school.

There is some indication that teachers are responsible for learning or not learning on the part of their students. The responsibility is met by force, not by inspiration or fairness. Also, it is evident that the counselee has not learned to think of learning as being self-initiated. He prefers Negro teachers and male teachers, not because they understand students, are more convivial, nor because he prefers his own race and sex, but because they are stricter and "make you work" so you learn more. To the best of his knowledge, the conditions for learning are those where someone forces your attention with some concern in order that you learn.

### School and Dropping Out

> I: If you were able to go through as far as you wanted, how far would you go?
> R: I'd go on through college.
> I: How come?
> R: *Just to make the goal. Just to do it.*
> I: How far do you think you'll actually go?
> R: I think on through.
> I: Why do you want to go . . . other than to play football?
> R: I just want to go there because Mr. L. (his history teacher) said if I do good I'll get a scholarship and it'd be easier.

It would appear from the above that school is really a marathon for the counselee, and the above again illustrates that the sole purpose is the task itself . . . just to make the goal. From the excerpts below, however, he doubts that he'll go to college:

> I: What else do you and he (father) agree on?
> R: A lot of things (?) like school he agrees that I should keep going.
> I: Do you feel the same way?
> R: Yes, he agrees that I should go to college but I don't feel the same about that part.
> I: What's your feeling about that?
> R: Going to college? I think that when I come out of the twelfth grade I'll be smart enough to do a good job.

It is difficult to determine what he thinks he's going to do a "good job" at for a long time. He never mentions it spontaneously. Still, he plans to take a college course at high school. He's not sure what kind of a college he wants to go to, the supposition being that he'll be thinking about this when he gets a little older. He knows that good grades and money are important to getting into college, however. He grasps the mechanics of the system and a means for making it (an athletic scholarship) without having any information or conception of what will go on in high school.

> I: Did you ever think of dropping out of school?
> R: No, I try to keep that out of my mind. Because I might start thinking about it and drop out.
> I: What keeps you from dropping out?
> R: My mother and father want me to make it, so I'm going to make it, or try to make it.
> I: What kind of things do you and she (mother) agree about?

R: School, too, that's the main subject, school. She wants me to get up there and learn. She don't want me to be like the rest of them, she's trying to get them to go back too but they won't. She don't want me to be like that.

I: Anything else?

R: No.

I: Well what kind of things do you and she disagree about?

R: We don't disagree about nothing except sometime I be kidding and say I ain't going to school and she'll talk to my father and then I get in trouble just for kidding around so I don't say that no more. I used to say it but I don't say it no more.

The counselee feels a lot of pressure from home about staying in school, since his older brothers dropped out and his parents did not finish high school. He really wants to finish "just to make the goal." He does express doubts about going to college, as his parents want him to do, and as he plans on very definitely. He tries not to think about quitting school, as he's afraid he might do it.

It is obvious that the counselee's guidance to date has been minimal. The counselee's confusions with respect to perceived educational and vocational options and alternatives suggest the need for extensive guidance assistance. The counselee needs information and guidance which will enable him to develop an increased awareness of his own preferred life style, learn how to translate his own college interests into practical educational realities, and learn to investigate work roles which are opening up for black people which will provide meaningful vocational opportunities.

### Example II

The following excerpts are from interview sessions with a 13-year-old high school freshman Negro boy, a good student. The counselee comes from a family of eight, six of whom are still at home.

#### Accuracy of What School Has to Offer and His Motives for Going There

The counselee is going to a Technical High School because his brother Sam is going there and his parents would like to see him there, too. The entrance examinations at Tech are difficult for most boys coming from the Junior High School that he came from, not only because of the testing situations, but because of the heavy emphasis on mathematics. The school secretary indicated that 2,000 boys took the entrance exam and only 500 were admitted this year. In the light of all this, the importance of his brother's example and his parents wishes seems very large, indeed. He does not say that he has chosen this school because of any particular training possibilities (which are available ) — but only that the family precedent leads him there. The counselee plans on taking a Business course at Tech, because he believes that this is necessary to go to college, where he would study engineering:

> I: What courses do you have to take in high school to get into college?
> R: You have to be in the Business course. I don't know what course you have to take.
> I: Business course, as opposed to what? Is there more than one course?
> R: There's Business course and Technical course is just the same as Business course, I think.

At the Technical High School, there are three courses: College, Technical, and Printing. The counselee is currently enrolled in the Printing course. There is no Business course. For a boy aspiring to be an engineer, Technical is the course in which he should be enrolled. It is evident that the counselee has not received any advice about his educational or occupational future as part of the school's guidance activities. The counselee is not aware of the possibilities for specialized training offered at the Technical High School. There may be some excuse for counseling at the junior high level not providing information on future work roles but there is no excuse for such poor management in handling information on high school curriculum options. Here is clearly an area of needed inputs of educational information and guidance.

> I: What do you have to do to become an engineer?
> R: Probably go to college.
> I: What kind of training do you need?
> R: Engineering training, I think.
> I: Where would you go to school for this?
> R: I'd go to Harvard. Or maybe Northeastern.
> I: Are you thinking of the service as a possibility for training?
> R: You can be an engineer in there.
> I: Would you consider this?
> R: No. I don't want to go to no military service.
> I: Why not?
> R: I don't know. I just don't want to go. It's boring.

---

> I: If your father could have been anything he wanted to be, what do you think he would have been?
> R: Tell you what he wanted to be — an electronic engineer.
> I: What stopped him from doing that?
> R: I don't know. He said something was wrong with his back. He went two years to college, then something happened to his back. Couldn't take it no more, he switched over to another course.

The counselee's father never finished high school, but later went back to take some high school night courses: this was all fairly recent. His father has also studied radio and TV repair by special courses. The counselee interprets this training as college. Although he has a clear idea of what college, in the traditional sense means, he also may use the term to denote extra or specialized training after the normal age for school attendance is over. The counselee says that his father learned to be a compressor mechanic in college. It is not exactly clear just when in his father's career that he went to college. The father held a variety of jobs — radio and TV repair was one (*often called "electronic engineer" by other boys who have been interviewed*).

### The Counselee's Perception of School

At first, the counselee says that Negro and white teachers treat and teach the kids the same, in general, but he goes on:

I: If you could be taught by mainly Negro teachers or mainly white teachers, which would you pick?
R: Negro teachers.
I: Why is that?
R: Because it's funny. If we've got white teachers I probably won't be able to pay attention.
I: Why not?
R: *Because they probably won't care.*

---

I: What do you think the teachers think of the kids?
R: Some, like Mr. B., he said, "We ought to lock these kids up. When we have classes, we ought to have them in jails, so they won't get away. We ought to have jails, or some kind of doors that just push you back in or something."
I: What about the other teachers? What do you think they think of the kids?
R: They don't care. Like this man teaches me, he says, "If they don't want to work, they flunk. If they want to work, they pass." He don't care.

He has particularly disliked his art, shop, and science teachers. The first two were boring and talked instead of getting down to teaching.

I: What's she like? (art teacher)
R: She hated me. 'Cause I hated her.
I: Why?
R: I don't know, she used to be a boring teacher. She just talk and talk and talk. And about five [minutes] before we went to lunch, she'd start work, and we'd be late for lunch. She was so boring.

> One time I'm going to walk out of there and she'll ask where I'm going and I'll say I'm going out to lunch.

I: What shop teacher did you have?

R: Mr. S.

I: What was it?

R: Drafting.

I: What kind of a man is he?

R: We have two periods a day — Tuesday — and we have him for about 1½ hours he talks about when he was in the merchant marines, and about ½ hour we start work. And we don't want to listen to his life and what he was doing in the war and the merchant marines. Nobody wanted to listen to that. That's why when Mr. K. — we used to stay up there and sit around talking and he used to come up there real mad 'cause we didn't go to his class.

I: What did you get in drafting?

R: He gave me an A—; he must have been off his mind to give me an A—.

In contrast to these teachers, the counselee has most liked Mr. R., his teacher in the 4th and 6th grades because: "He was a reasonable teacher. He understands when you talk to him and try to help you out." Mr. M., his current algebra teacher, takes his free period to help students with their math problems. As contrasted with those teachers who "don't care if you pass or flunk."

Teachers, according to the counselee, fall into two general categories: those who are strict and have a "jailer" attitude, and those who "don't care." The first group according to the counselee are very clear as to who is "boss." The counselee thinks there should be more teachers like this, although the strictness must be tempered with concern. The teachers who "don't care" are those who are not concerned with whether the student passes or flunks.

The problem here is the reluctance of many teachers to try to reach and communicate with all their students and to try to adjust instruction to serve individual needs. To promote a guidance point of view and to encourage desirable educational change, the counselor must consider how teacher attitudes can be changed either through conferences with teachers or through special attention on an individual teacher basis.

### School and Dropping Out

Both the counselee and his parents are very insistent upon his finishing high school. He has no doubts that he can finish high school, although he is not quite as certain about college.

I: How far do your teachers think you should or could go in school?

R: All the way, if I pay attention.

I: How far do they think you'll actually go?

R: All the way.

I: How far does your mother think you should or could go in school?

R: She wants me to go all the way.

I: What about your father?

R: Him, too.

I: When you say "all the way", what do you mean?

R: Finish.

I: What?

R: *High school, and maybe go on to college.*

I: How far does he think you'll actually go?

R: All the way. *He's going to make me go all the way.*

I: Is there any one person in particular who you think has a special interest in how well you do in school?

R: My brother Sam. He don't want me to be a slob like him. He got kept back. He said "I hope you pass this year." 'Cause he flunk this year, and I'll be in the same grade he will. He used, *he don't want me to be like him. Be a slob.* He said "you might pass me or you might not."

I: Sam's at Technical?

R: Yes.

I: What do they say about your schoolwork?

R: They say, "Keep this up. You just might play basketball or go to college."

I: Now if you were able to go as far in school as you wanted to, how far would you go?

R: I'm finishing. Have some money to go to college, go to college, too.

I: Why?

R: I don't know why. *I just don't want to be no bum, with no money in my pocket.*

I: How far do you think you're likely to go?

R: I'll probably finish high school, but I might not go to college.

I: Why will you finish high school?

R: *I don't want no cheap job.*

I: Would anything prevent you from going to college?

R: Not that I know of.

I: Do you ever think of dropping out of school?

R: No.

I: Why not?

R: I don't know. My sister said "You drop out, you make a big mistake."

I: Which one?

R: Thelma.

I: And what does she say about it?

R: She said if she didn't drop out of school, she might be living all on her own.

The above makes abundantly clear that being a success in school is being a success as an individual. Sam thinks he's a "slob" for having flunked. Thelma could be "on her own." Jobs which do not require schooling are "cheap." The good jobs to which he aspires, jobs that require education, are engineering and professional athletics. In earlier interviews he has indicated that engineers make money, are prestigious, and have positions of power and responsibility, requiring skill. Basketball players are "strong." They don't "fall apart" and people watch them. The counselee is trying to become a man, and he sees school as being an important part of his realizing this ideal.

No real interest in an occupation has resulted from his classroom experiences, however, except that he likes math and math is involved in engineering. The connection here, however, is not causal. To date, his school experiences have not formed a part of his view of the work-world. His aspirations for particular jobs stem from his family and the mass media, and his desire to remain in school is related to his family only.

The above information suggests that the counselee's perception of his environment and the reality of education and work requirements are not as tenuous as that of the first counselee. He does value education and understands the social and economic importance of work. Occupational inputs must be provided that not only increase the counselee's general awareness of occupational areas and career ladders but teach the counselee to develop planning strategies which will aid him in organizing information about himself and the world of work and enable him to develop the alternatives and options that will be necessary if he is to be successful in implementing his choices.

In summary, this information gathering technique on the part of the general practitioner will serve a dual purpose. First, it will assure that the questions of pressures on the individual to achieve, the paths available to his achievement, and the values that the individual ascribes to achieving will now become open questions from the guidance point of view with no stigma attached. Second, it will assure growth and development on the part of the practitioner as well as on the part of the student. The practitioner can profit from each of these experiences of seeing the individual on his own terms and in so doing arrive at wider consensual realities to serve as the base from which he makes determinations as to appropriate guidance actions.

# 5

# New Information Devices and Methods for Effecting Change

Clarification of the rationale for the use of educational and vocational information must take place within the complex of the sociological, economic, and cultural changes that are taking place today. It was suggested earlier that a major reason for a youth's failure to cope with the adult environment is in-school lack of confidence in his own ability to control any aspect of his environment and a devastating lack of knowledge of how education, as a tool rather than as a credential, can be used in real life to move him toward his own real goals.

Therefore, in the development of vocational guidance technology and the application of methods and techniques the author has been prone to stress the importance of treating guidance as a learning process. Action must be taken to make guidance integral to the total educational effort, and materials and procedures must be designed and developed to be responsive to the types of learning and learning skills an individual will need for self-management at any given period of his school and out-of-school growth and development.

The question now arises as to how we can improve our guidance information and communications so that they are responsive to the needs of today's youth (such as the two youths described in the preceding chapter) and will assist these youngsters to become more effective and

49

forceful individuals with some sense of identity in a complex, technological world.

Education has become more and more artificial in relation to youth's real world of experience. Specifically, youth has become more and more alienated from the physical world of work. Few children see or observe any workers other than the classroom teachers. They tend to know little about real work chances in their own community, let alone outside their community. Teachers know little of the role of the trade unions which control about one-fourth of the jobs in the country nor the specialty careers open in the armed forces (often the only escape ladder for the intelligent but deprived youngster), and not the least, youth today lives in a society that itself is puzzled about how to cope with advancing automation. In addition, McLeish (1967), Rosenthal (1966a), and others have pointed out that youngsters today are seeking personal effectiveness and meaningful group relationships, and are looking to participate in experiences which will contribute to their sense of identity and effectiveness and permit them to establish and maintain interpersonal bonds and relationships with each other and the community.

It is obviously impossible in this monograph to illustrate all types of materials and media which may be used in counseling interviews, small-group counseling, or classroom situations. When providing information on these formidable problems facing today's youth, the guidance practitioner should use information in more imaginative ways than the mere handing out of factual printed material.

In the sections that follow, major ways in which the counselor might use information in communicating with youth will be discussed and ways in which these information devices fit into a developmentally-oriented system for guidance will be stressed. These techniques and methods will be described in terms of the structure of the components of the Information-Learning model presented in Chapter 3 although emphasis will be on practical applications.

First, however, the pertinent question of whether to use direct or simulated experiences will be examined and clarified.

### Direct vs. Simulated Experiences

Roeber (1966) has stressed the need to bring about some balance in the curriculum between the introduction of direct and simulated experiences relative to the student's readiness for certain types of information. Katz (1966) notes that although acquisition of information through direct experiences is desirable in some respects, it also carries undesirable concomitants. He states that:

The counselor may wish to provide a high school student direct experience in the work world in connection with some specific occupational area. However, this specific experience enables the student to sample very, very sparingly from the physical, social, intellectual, and emotional demands of the vocational area to which he is exposed. For example, if the student obtains an after school or summer job, the specific conditions of the job itself, the specific supervisor he works under, the specific place and pressures of the job, the specific individuals he works with may be representative of that occupation as a whole, but may also be idiosyncratic. It is difficult under these circumstances to provide the student with a sense of proportion in judging which elements from this direct work experience are what might be called reliable samples of the total occupational area — the total type of experience the counselor would like him to have — and which are simply error.

Therefore a worthwhile consideration and desirable direction has been to put in capsule or simulation form the various types of direct experiences that the counselor would like a student to have. These simulation techniques may involve the use of audio-visual methods, gaming devices, computers, and other techniques of one sort or another. They should not sacrifice the essential qualities of direct experience but at the same time should exclude a lot of the "noise." In designing these simulated situations it is important that they do not become too artificial but have the attributes of realistic situations in which the student can engage in tasks and develop a range of skills and learning techniques that will be useful to him in real life.

Thus, simulated experience is necessary where students in a complex society cannot have direct experiences with all people, ideas, and things that are or will be significant to them. Whether or not changes in the student's behavior occur as a result of these simulated experiences will depend in large part on the support and reinforcement the student receives in the course of his attending to such tasks, the sensory appeal, and meaningful qualities of the types of vicarious experiences presented, and to what extent the experiences are planned in a developmental framework of increasing complexity and significance. The guidance specialist must design the simulated experiences as elements of a total realistic experience in order that the individual can then relate the insight acquired from the series of experiences to perceived or experienced situations that he is aware of and recognizes as part of the real world.

Two broad categories of performance learning have been generally identified in the literature and have been included in the structure of the Information-Learning Model in Chapter 3. These two major categories of learning include: (1) broadening vocational awareness, and (2) establishing vocational planning and problem-solving skills. What kinds of experiences, both direct and simulated, should be provided for youth in our schools to effect these important kinds of change? To help in answering this question, the types of materials and methods that might be employed for these purposes are considered in the sections that follow.

## Increasing Occupational Awareness Through The Use of Conceptual Schemes

Informational materials based on conceptual schemes provide the individual with an organized way of viewing himself in relation to his environment. Therefore, in providing information for increasing personal and vocational awareness, the guidance specialist would do well to make use of materials that employ conceptual schemes, behavioral models, or themes that are relevant to ascertained information needs of the student. The fundamental information needs of the student include: to know more about himself as a human being capable of choice; to know more about education as a system of vocational training and development (without regard to subject matter); and to know more about the realities of the world of home, community, and work.

Unfortunately, the concentration of effort in the development of information has been primarily in the area of generic concepts and specific facts regarding occupations and work. Little attention has been devoted to developing information on education; and concentration on information that implements the development of the self-concept has been almost nonexistent. Since most of the materials currently available have concentrated on providing information on occupations and work, we will discuss these materials first. Following are some examples of vocational information materials that are organized on the basis of schemes of work, education, and self-awareness that could provide the student with a useful way of "coding" information for planning and goalsetting.

### The Functional Structure of the New DOT

The third edition of the *Dictionary of Occupational Titles,* 1965, (DOT) provides a natural base for the development of a conceptual framework for the world of work, emphasizing a functional approach to the analysis of work. The job classification scheme utilized by the new DOT is based on the concept of Worker Functions. Worker Functions arise in connection with the way a worker relates to People, Data, and Things, and can be described in terms of a hierarchy or graded continuum of classes of tasks. By assessing a job along each hierarchy, a profile of Worker Functions is obtained for each job. These profiles can then be grouped or "clustered" according to jobs which have similar People-Data-Thing characteristics. The DOT then describes these clusters in terms of similarity of Worker Traits (e.g., general educational development, training time, aptitudes, temperaments, physical demands, and working conditions) required by the worker categorized according to the industry with which the occupation is usually affiliated.

It is important that the practitioner recognize that he should not use this scheme to advise or sort the student into an area of work to which he belongs. In the design of the DOT, the Labor Department utilized a trait-factor approach to relate job information to particular patterns of interests, abilities, and levels of educational attainment. This practice of profile matching for selection and recruitment purposes should be avoided at all costs by the counselor as he utilizes this information in his guidance activities with students, because it implies that he should find a match for the student with a particular job or type of job.

Notwithstanding, the conceptual scheme of the DOT provides an interesting and useful model for the student to learn to apply in exploring and investigating the world of occupations in terms of Worker Functions (what workers do) and Worker Traits. However, the guidance specialist must be prepared to identify or devise materials and methods suitable for teaching students how to use this scheme as a "coding" device so that the information will take on personal meaning as the student learns to apply the scheme for his own purposes.

Pertinent to this discussion are practical examples and illustrations of specific ways in which a functional approach to work may be utilized by the guidance practitioner in his efforts to broaden vocational awareness.

### Learning to Utilize Functional Concepts of Work

The feedback that one often gets from counselors in connection with providing information on jobs using materials based on the DOT is, "Do I have to know everything that's in the *Dictionary of Occupational Titles?*" or "Do I have to know everything that's in the *Occupational Outlook Handbook?*" Of course they don't — It would be impossible in any case. No one counselor can be expected to know all about every occupation in the complex world in which we live.

To successfully utilize the occupational structure of the DOT, whether presented in print, on microfilm, or on film, the counselor or guidance practitioner needs to understand first and foremost the ways in which jobs serve as vehicles for human beings to express themselves, to satisfy their needs, and to satisfy the requirements of the jobs. The best orientation and framework for this understanding is through a thorough grounding in the functional concepts of work. Fine (1964, 1967) has developed several publications on this subject that should prove extremely valuable to counselors in comprehending these concepts and applying them when setting up an information program on work.

To rephrase this point of view, the counselor has to be able to relate the dimensions of jobs such as those described by the functional constructs of the DOT to the student's experience, his responses, and his sensitivities as a human being. In working with individuals and groups, the counselor needs to understand and interpret the student's experience in terms of its implications for the work situation. Following are some suggestions on how such translations for the student might be made.

To make occupational information meaningful to the student, this must be communicated to him: When a person goes to his job, he goes there as a whole person. He doesn't just take a part of himself there. His body is there, his mind is there, his personality is there; all of himself as a person is there. In order to communicate this information to the student the counselor will need to capitalize on both direct and simulated experiences that can provide the student with ideas of the main things that workers are called upon to do; like using their bodies, hands, and legs, to work with *things;* using their minds to work with *information;* using their personalities to get things done with *people.* It is also necessary that these experiences communicate the cognitive information — the task to be performed increases in complexity, the instructions to be followed become more complicated. Also, as the amount of judgment needed on the job increases, the more the worker is left on his own, and this requires more knowledge and experience.

To accomplish these kinds of learnings, the counselor must arrange to have the student look at jobs or job models where the aspects of work are communicated in functional terms. This may be accomplished either vicariously through the use of film material, or directly through visits and field trips, part-time jobs, by interviewing workers, or through duplicating actual work conditions in the vocational program of the school.

To aid the student in looking at the functional aspects of jobs, the information program might include materials that describe simple forms of work and then progress to the more complex. In the course of the program, the student should gradually understand the following:

1. Some jobs use simple tools; jobs such as clam digging, sweeping, and cleaning. There isn't much leeway for judgment in these jobs.
2. Some jobs consist primarily of working with machinery. Simpler

jobs of this sort consist of feeding things into machines or taking things that have already been made from machines. The more complex jobs consist of starting, stopping, and making adjustments in the controls of the machinery. For example, there is more to lubricating a car than polishing a car; there is more to being a railroad brakeman and doing switching work than digging a ditch. These latter jobs are more precise, more specific, more measured. There isn't very much room for judgment, but there is a lot of detail with which the worker should be concerned.

3. There is a big difference between the knowledge and skill required in operating different kinds of equipment. It takes different amounts of training for one worker to do a particular job than for another.

4. It takes trained and experienced hands to manage tools on skilled jobs such as that of plumber, dressmaker, or dental hygienist. Such jobs call for considerable judgment and these workers have a lot of leeway in the way they do their jobs.

Students should look at the difference in the controls of equipment when they are on field visits. Counselors should try to have them see jobs in which a worker has to set up his machine; that is, adjust and arrange the devices that control the speed and depth of a cut, the amount of lubricant fed to the material so that it won't overheat, and things of that nature. It would also be helpful for students to see jobs of people who set up machines for other workers, such as data processing and computing machinery. They should look at the tools and the equipment that people work with on their jobs, realizing that there is room in the world for new ideas about how to get the job done. There is even room for them to invent new ways of doing things.

In other words, when students are taken on field trips to look at jobs they should notice how each person is functioning on the job. If the students have an opportunity to ask questions of the people there, the questions should be geared to find out what the worker does. For example: Does the worker set up the machine? Does he make adjustments to the machine? Does he maintain it — keep it in operating condition? Does somebody else maintain it? Who calls the maintenance man? In this way, students will get an understanding of the worker's "things" involvement.

If the worker's job is primarily in the data area, the students might be able to find out where the worker gets his instructions. How much leeway is there in that instruction? What type of machines or equipment does he use? Does he set up the machine himself? Does he determine his own sequence of operation? Does he decide which material to get; how much material to get? Does he decide when work has reached standard specifications? Who inspects it? How much thinking does he have to do?

Then as far as people-related jobs are concerned: How often does the worker see a supervisor? What are the worker relations required with his peers, with his co-workers? If students approach the jobs they view with this functional framework in mind they will not only be better able to compare one job with another but the jobs will take on more real meaning for them in terms of activities (functions) that can be related to their own experience.

### Learning to Utilize Concepts of Job Satisfaction

In providing information on work, practitioners must also take into consideration the affective domain of understanding. Educators like to talk about the *needs* of students, and counselors know that their wants and needs are expressed or manifested in very simple and ordinary ways. A disadvantaged child, because of his experiences at home, is probably most anxious about security; particularly anxious in ways in which it is difficult for those who have resolved many of these needs — for security, for shelter, for the integrity of the person, for help — to understand. These wants and needs express themselves in very simple language and most counselors could probably provide some wonderful anecdotes from their experiences.

Other children exhibit a tremendous need for recognition — a response of some kind from other people. This shows up in the way they tend to be followers. They tend to want to be shown. They attach themselves to teachers. They attach themselves to friends. People like this generally have satisfied their need for security, physical shelter, and what they need is a sense of personal security coming from the response of others.

Then there is the need for achievement, for self-realization. This need is typically found in authors, but also in various kinds of professional people — engineers, research psychologists, etc. These individuals don't care really about anything else except realizing themselves in terms of what they wish to achieve.

Such needs translate themselves into definite actualities in work. When you have students examine the employment conditions under which individuals work or when you have them talk to personnel officers as to the concerns of the worker, they will find that these needs are the things that people are most concerned with on the job. Workers are concerned with pay and with fringe benefits; with basic conditions in the plant; with management providing work; and with management providing workmen's compensation. Some workers are very concerned about security. Then there are the individuals who try to design their jobs so that they can be achievers. They are simply interested in those circumstances of their work, the support circumstances, that permit them to be achievers and that give them recognition as achievers. Self-realization as an engineer, as a scientist, as a creative person is another way of looking at work.

What has been presented above are job satisfaction factors (security, social recognition, self-realization) that counselors have to understand every time they look at a job. If counselors do not think of jobs in these terms then all they see is a confusion of machinery — smells, sights, sounds — a set of isolated tasks. They see motions of workers perhaps, and then talk to students about so much training and so little training, or so much education or so little education, without really understanding what is going on in the world of work.

In summary, the focus of a student's perceptions, when he is exposed to information on work, when he is taken on a visit to an industrial plant as part of a guidance program, or when someone is brought from industry to talk to him should be on two things: (1) how the worker functions on the job in terms of people, data, and things, and (2) the type of satisfaction he can derive from his work to fulfill his wants and needs.

### Materials Based On Functional Concepts of Work

Let us now consider several types of materials that utilize the conceptual scheme of the DOT for the presentation of occupational information.

#### Viewscripts of Occupational Facts

Information on specific jobs using the conceptual schemes of the DOT has been simplified and made available to students by microfilm and audio-visual aids. Viewscripts (VIEW) is an example of this method of communication. This approach grew out of a recognized need (in San Diego County, California) to provide students with accurate, up-to-date information regarding local training and occupational opportunities in that area. The occupational information is gathered by combining national, regional, and state publications with educational-occupational community surveys. Special microfilm machines enable the student to view the material by himself, select those parts he wants, and obtain a reproduction of the information he wants through a simple mechanical device. As local and regional occupational information is subject to rapid change, the counseling office can easily update the information by making up new typed copies of current information and converting it to microfilm. This system is now being adopted and used in other sections of the country. One of its greatest advantages is that it gives an inexpensive way of making factual occupational information widely available.

Several by-products of the original scheme have become an integral part of the information program. For example, the VIEW system allows the counselor to learn by student actions what is important to the student. The primary problem seems to be associated with bridging the gap between student use of the microfilm and counseling interviews between students and counselors. It is the danger of the gimmick being used as a possible substitute for professional counseling.

### *"Life Style" Films on Work*

In making use of the conceptual framework of the functional analysis of work what kind of open skills do we want to provide the student? Martin's intention was to broaden the individual's awareness of life style as projected in work as it relates to values and aspirations and quality of living as well as vocational competence for a job. To do this she developed several life style films on workers that utilized the functional model of the DOT. Earlier studies by Martin (1967) indicated the effectiveness of the use of the media for guidance purposes.

These generic concepts of work are stimulated by showing the group a film depicting a man at work, who represents a person fulfilling a complete life style, the type of satisfactions that result from his work plus some of his goals and aspirations. This film stimulates the generic concept of work by communicating to the individual the following:

1. Identifies the three basic components of work: people, data, things.
2. Demonstrates the skill requirements that exist in work.
3. Demonstrates the training requirements that exist in work.
4. Identifies the interpersonal and supervisory relations that exist in work.
5. Demonstrates that work allows a person to fulfill a life style.
6. Demonstrates the satisfactions that result from work.
7. Establishes respect for the social as well as the economic value of work.

Through the dynamics of group discussion that follow the use of the material, the concepts introduced are broadened for the individual student and thus greatly reinforced. This material is being made available commercially through Mar-Media, Inc., Pittsburgh, Pennsylvania.

### *Widening Occupational Roles Kit*

It is to be assumed that once students have acquired an understanding of the concept of life style in work, more cognitive type learnings can take place. Lifton's Widening Occupational Roles Kit for grades six through nine is designed to enable students to explore career opportunities in functional terms and see the interdependence of all occupations. The materials also pinpoint the extent of education needed to prepare for the occupation of their choice. Guidance booklets and filmstrips introduce various topics (e.g., "Planning for the Future") for class discussion or individual research. Workbooks are provided for students to use in recording their abilities, interests, achievements, hobbies, and so forth. Once the student has considered these areas, he can then turn to the Job Briefs that describe 400 separate jobs in detail to find the occupational field that best suits him. These materials may be obtained from Science Research Associates, Inc., Chicago, Illinois.

## Occupational Problem-Solving Kits

In the way of media, Krumboltz has developed sets of occupational problem-solving kits for use by students and has tested several alternative ways of constructing and using these materials. Studies conducted by Krumboltz and associates (Hamilton and Krumboltz, 1969; Bergland and Krumboltz, 1969) have investigated the effectiveness of these kits and other counseling materials for broadening the students' awareness of vocational areas. The results indicate that the materials must be tailored to suit the interests, motivations, and ability levels of the students. These materials are being made available through Science Research Associates, Inc., Chicago, Illinois.

## Ohio Vocational Interest Survey (OVIS)

The OVIS is a new interest inventory designed to assist students in grades eight through twelve with their educational and vocational plans. The inventory makes use of a data-people-things model of the world of work to define the domain of vocational interests. The OVIS is compatible with the philosophy of self-direction by students and is suited for group and individual exploration of the world of work.

The interest inventory provides profiles of a student's interests along 24 scales. These scales represent the entire spectrum of occupations as defined in the new DOT. Thus, the interest scores can be interpreted in terms of actual jobs that a student may wish to investigate. In addition, the OVIS provides a student questionnaire to provide the student and his counselor with background data for interpreting the student's interest scores. A schoolwide summary of the questionnaire can furnish useful information for planning guidance services and curriculum changes. These materials are being published by Harcourt, Brace and World, Inc., Test Department, New York.

*Televised Programs of Local Job Opportunities*

Many large school systems are producing their own television materials on job opportunities available locally. These materials have not been specifically designed on the functional approach of the DOT but do provide definite factual information on a variety of occupational areas.

An audio-visual technique that has been used for guidance in the Atlanta, Georgia public school system consists of a weekly television series depicting jobs in 36 different areas. Occupational areas featured in the programs have included health careers, education, aircraft manufacturing, banking, retailing, catalog sales, telephone industry, construction, air transportation, bus transportation, trucking industry, petroleum industry, railroads, social service, engineers, armed forces, and newspaper publishing. The series, *Countdown to the 70's,* initiated by the Occupational Information Materials project of the Atlanta Public Schools, is designed to disseminate accurate occupational information to students in Atlanta's upper elementary and middle grades (6th, 7th, 8th) in order that they may obtain a broader knowledge of all phases of the world of work.

Selections for program content were based on children's expressed interests, U.S. Department of Labor forecasts of future employment opportunities, community resources, and training facilities. The supplementary materials for classroom use include lesson guides with suggested activities for preparation and follow-up, posters (drawn by staff artist) showing workers featured on telecasts, booklets containing job descriptions of workers shown on the program — including definitions of their duties, personal qualifications, and training. This shows what a school system might do in the way of communicating specific occupational information to its student body.

### Increasing Educational Awareness

The materials discussed above show how different media (print, microfilm, and videotape) have been used to broaden vocational awareness and communicate specific occupational information to individuals or groups. But there is also a need to communicate information on education. While this need may often be adequately met for college-bound youth, the availability of such information for noncollege-bound youth is often minimal. Several efforts to correct this situation are illustrated below. Unfortunately, little headway has been made in conceptualizing the theoretical aspects and functional concepts of education for the purposes of guidance analogous to those accomplished in describing the functional concepts of work.

### The Specialty Oriented Student Program (SOS)

The SOS program, designed and developed by Hoyt, is an attempt to aid the counselor in providing guidance information geared to students planning to enter trade, technical, or business training institutions. The rationale on which this material (booklets for students) is based is that occupational information generally concentrates too much attention on answering questions deemed pertinent by experts in labor market information and too little attention on questions which students are asking as they attempt to make educational and vocational decisions. The educational information in the booklets concentrates on characteristics and experiences of students in training (e.g., what kinds of people enroll in these programs, where these students live, what their evaluation is of the instructors). The occupational information concentrates on what happens to people in the occupations thus answering the question, "What is likely to happen to me if I pursue this training program and enter this occupation?"

Distributions of actual responses of students in these programs are provided to these questions rather than absolute answers to allow the counselee to think in terms of possibilities and probabilities. The designers of the material suggest that direct use may be made of the materials during the counseling interview and that this is congruent with the purposes of the information. This material may be obtained through the Bureau of Educational Research, University of Iowa, Iowa City, Iowa.

### Audiovisual Information on Vocational and Technical Education

The Division of Guidance and Testing, Ohio State Department of Education has produced a series of filmstrips oriented around the general theme of helping high school students recognize the relationships between vocational education and occupational choice. This project began with one filmstrip entitled "Your Future Through Technical Education" produced in cooperation with Ohio State University. Currently, the series has been extended to a variety of topics on vocational education and emerging occupations and the filmstrips are now being published and distributed commercially. These filmstrips are designed to provide information to students who will not attend college, in order to make them more aware of their needs for and opportunities in public school vocational-technical education programs at the high school and post-high school level.

The filmstrips are intended for use by individual students and/or in group guidance activities at the junior and senior high school level and are short enough to fit into a regular school schedule. It is anticipated that as a result of their use, students will be motivated to seek individual counseling — therefore, they should be used as part of a planned program of guidance services. This material may be obtained from Guidance Associates, Pleasantville, New York.

### Televised Information for Educational Planning

An example of the use of audiovisual materials for educational planning is that of the program developed and utilized by "Project You" in the Dade County, Florida schools. "Project You" describes one of its goals as making students see a personal meaning for school opportunities so that they can arrive at realistic educational-vocational plans. To accomplish this, eighth graders participate in a two-week program consisting of "telelessons" and booklets containing written assignments and ideas for discussion. The first four lessons are concerned with "vocational exploration" — the necessity of planning for a vocation, of knowing special interests and abilities, of knowing how personality and attitudes affect jobs. The latter six lessons deal with "educational exploration" — graduation requirements, curricula available, and opportunities in Dade County for post-high school training. The aim is to motivate students to think in terms of their abilities and interests, the world of self, and relate this thinking to the worlds of education and work.

### Computer-Based Educational-Occupational Guidance Data System

An example of a promising computer-based educational-occupational guidance data system in actual operation in the schools is the Interactive College Suggesting System and Career Training Information System, Concord-Carlisle, High School, Massachusetts. This system provides students with current information on schools and colleges. A teletypewriter terminal in the Guidance Department is connected by phone with the Interactive Learning Systems data banks in Boston.

The student uses the terminal to interact with the data bank listing over 3,000 colleges and universities across the country. With the assistance of the counselor, the student must first decide which of the 300 characteristics on the worksheet provided by the system are important to him. These characteristics include geographical location, size of student body, majors available, average SAT or ACT scores, and costs. When this information is submitted to the system, the student receives a print-out or listing of schools meeting his criteria. The counseling process continues with the student discussing alternatives during interview sessions with his counselor. He is also encouraged to discuss these matters with his parents. Gradually the student arrives at a more objective appraisal of possibilities on which he can act.

### Increasing Self Awareness through Humanistic Guidance

Unfortunately, the prevailing tendency has been to keep the *psychological* and *sociological* aspects of information *separate* from the *occupational* aspects. Responsible guidance information programs, however, must have a dual objective: to promote the developmental process of occupational choice, and to provide content and technique for adjustive guidance. These dual objectives must be met if the program is to be successful in aiding the individual to accomplish the transition from school to adult and work life.

To date, the major emphasis in educational and vocational information has been placed on materials that stress the needs of students for choice of college or for identifying vocational opportunities open to them. Very little attention has been devoted to materials that involve the youngster in a search for personal identity and increased awareness of self and others. This is despite the continual stress that vocational development theorists have placed on the complementary relationship of the self-concept and occupational information in the developmental process of occupational choice.

To fill this gap, Martin (1970) has embarked on a program of development and implementation of a curriculum series of "slice of life" film modules that are proving to be effective media utilizing a developmental and humanistic approach to guidance. These models are drawn from theoretical and empirical vocational development research. The models utilized have been based on constructs of Gribbons' and Lohnes' *Readiness for Vocational Planning* (1966), Rosenthal's *Pathways to Identity* (1966b), and Fine's *Functional Concepts of Work* (1955).

The following constitutes a specific example of the practice of the technique in the motivation of individuals with respect to the generic concepts of self and individual differences. Generic and specific concepts of education and work have also been treated.

The aspects of self and individual differences are stimulated by showing a group of students a series of situational "slice of life" films exhibiting a "typical" day in the lives of recent high school graduates and high school students. The behavioral elements of the film correspond to the theoretical aspects of self. This media is primarily focused on the ways in which individuals differ. Specifically, the vocational awareness aspect is stimulated by communicating to the individual the differences among various individuals and how each is behaving in the high school or adult environment; aiding the individual to identify and recognize the requirements that are essential to the adult environment and that the student will soon have to face; providing the individual with an opportunity to appraise himself in relation to these requirements; and affording the individual an opportunity to become aware of characteristics inherent in himself and his environment that enter into individual planning and choice.

In the practice of this technique the guidance practitioner does not teach concepts, attitudes, or beliefs; instead he permits the model stimulus materials to stimulate the students to respond to the ideas in their own words. Group discussion is the vehicle through which the concepts stimulated by the elements of the film material are reinforced and become meaningful to the individual. Knowledge of attributes of the concepts is broadened by group interaction.

An important feedback device for the student is the audiorecording of the individual student response. Tape recordings of the discussion are used by the students during the course of the program as they provide an auditory record for the student to evaluate his own growth and development. In addition, the tape recording may be used by the guidance practitioner to learn more about the motivations and understandings of the student and the types of information he now needs. These materials may be obtained from Mar Media, Inc., Pittsburgh, Pa.

### Developing Problem-Solving and Decision-Making Skills

Katz (1963) has indicated that the major role of guidance is to reduce the discrepancy between a student's untutored readiness for rational behavior and some hypothetical ideal state of knowledge and wisdom. In considering information generally, regardless of any single career-development state he has noted the following:

> Decision-making . . . may be regarded as a strategy for acquiring and processing information. If a decision is truly *to be made,* if it is not a foregone conclusion, it must involve some novel elements. The person confronted with the problem of decision-making either does not know what information he needs, does not have what information he wants, or cannot use what information he has. Thus, the pressure for making a decision creates a discrepancy between the individual's present state of knowledge (or wisdom) and the state that is being demanded of him.

Wrenn (1962) also has viewed the priority task of guidance as that of helping students to develop and use skills which enable them to plan, make, and implement decisions wisely. Wrenn has noted that many of the problems faced by youth in today's world have become more complex (e.g., choosing an occupation) or have recently come into existence (e.g., use of leisure time). He believes that this trend toward new problems and the increasing complexity of old ones is likely to continue, perhaps even at an accelerated pace in the future.

There is no doubt that the conceptual base for occupational information should include development of skills of inquiry and problem-solving ability that are generally applicable to a wide range of real-life problems that the individual will face in managing his own life. Several types of training materials and simulated devices developed to prepare secondary school students to make educational-vocational decisions are provided below. The theoretical and practical considerations on which these materials and programs are based differ considerably.

### Vocational Guidance Materials for Planning and Problem Solving

#### You: Today and Tomorrow

A booklet with which students work was conceived by Katz and exemplifies an early attempt to develop guidance material to be used in planning and decision-making skills (Katz, 1959). This book-let is appropriate for eighth or ninth grade students. Its format makes it most suitable for precollegiate youth. The program's approach em-phasizes the student's need for self-appraisal for educational and vocational planning which should take place prior to or at the begin-ning of the individual's high school education. The booklet primarily discusses abilities, values, and interests, examining how they work to-gether or conflict, how they are related to goals, and how they influence a choice of occupations and education. Illustrations, checklists, and questionnaires stimulate the interest and participation of the student and are designed so that the student can begin to appraise himself in terms of abilities and interests and develop a more consistent set of values in choice and decision-making. This material is available through Educational Testing Service, Princeton, New Jersey.

#### The Life Career Game

Developed by Boocook (John Hopkins University), this game is an example of a simulation technique for vocational guidance. It simulates all of the major features of the type of environment that students will face as they mature. Students plan the life of a fictitious youth with respect to his education, occupation, family life, and leisure, allocating various amounts of time to various endeavors. Players de-termine both the different activities of the youth and the amount of attention he devotes to them. The goal of the game is to attain a life "satisfaction" score that is as high as possible. Decisions are made in rounds, each round representing a year in the youth's life. At the end of each round, data based on national samples indicate the probabilities of certain things occurring, with chance built in by the use of spinner and dice. It is expected that students who participate in the *Life Career Game* will gain insight into the concept that probabilities are associated with choices and that this knowledge will transfer to the decision-making process in the adult environment. The operations and procedures of the game are somewhat complex, a factor which may tend to limit its usefulness with less motivated and less talented youth.

## Self-Directed Learning Program

Magoon (1968) has also been interested in improving the problem-solving behavior of college students. Over a period of years, Magoon has developed and put into operation a guidance model for counseling college students best described as a self-directed learning program which makes use of audiorecording and audiotapes. The program teaches the individual the steps to be taken in effective problem-solving and focuses in particular on vocational indecision problems of college students. The model is quite structured in sequence and format and requires the student to produce written responses to a series of carefully arranged questions. The counselors' role is one of reviewing and assessing the student's progress, planning next steps, and initiating motivation.

### Training for Decision Making

## Invitation to Decision

The emphasis of the counseling and guidance program in the Palo Alto, California public schools (under the general direction of Gellatt) is upon assisting students in the decision-making process. Materials and techniques developed and used in the guidance program have been devised to teach the students the actual process of educational-vocational decision-making. For example: *Invitation to Decision* is a workbook that is used along with visual aids and other relevant materials including the *Life Career Game* and computer-assisted counseling. These materials form the basis for a series of group guidance sessions presented to all ninth and eleventh grade students. In addition to pertinent information about the decision-making process and about high school and college, the decision workbook contains "experience tables" that report the experiences of former Palo Alto students while in high school and following graduation. It is expected that the student will learn to interpret these facts in light of his own abilities and interests in planning his high school courses and future career. The school system reports some evidence that decision-making with respect to educational choice is more effective for students utilizing the workbook in relation to their own personal data such as grade-point-average and test scores. The format of the materials and of the program, in general, is most suitable for precollegiate youth. These materials are not being distributed commercially; however, there is the possibility that they may be obtained from the Palo Alto Guidance Department and adapted for local use.

### Computer-Based Training Models

Several comprehensive programs for computer-based training systems for vocational decision-making have been developed and are being tried experimentally in various school systems (Cogswell, 1967; Super, 1969; and Tiedeman, 1967). These computer-based systems range from those designed primarily for retrieval of educational and vocational information to those that will be combined with a model course in vocational decision-making and individualized guidance from the counselor.

Areas of concern that the developers of these systems have been working upon include: broadening the data base used by these systems to include additional kinds of information on education, training, and jobs; expanding the personal data file on users of the system; devising dialogue systems for use with computers which permit freely constructed questions; and developing training techniques for counselors which will enable them to interpret the computer print-outs of probability information profiles.

### Summary

In summary, the kind of emphasis for vocational information and guidance that has been presented in these chapters is relatively new. What has been suggested is that the focus of guidance information method and technique should change from a fascination with how to predict the probability of success of individuals or how to match the characteristics of individuals, educational programs, and jobs, to what guidance practitioners need to know to help youth develop the understanding by which to manage their own lives more realistically and rationally.

Stress has been placed throughout this monograph on the need for guidance to be viewed developmentally rather than as a specific act of providing information for vocational choice. Several steps have been proposed for the implementation of information in guidance with this emphasis in mind. First, the guidance practitioner should develop in an objective, empirical manner, a valid set of perceptual understanding of what children and youth are like and what the group is like that he will be dealing with in a given community. Second, the practitioner should look carefully for theory on which the design of his information program and practice will be based so that he will not find himself at the mercy of every fad and fancy that comes along. Third, the practitioner should specify (as difficult a task as this may be) the kinds of changes (outcomes) his system is designed to produce and the technology that he will bring to bear. Last, the practitioner should identify a pool of methods, materials and techniques from which he can proceed with greater competence to help a youngster over a developmental period to realize his goals or become a dignified member of a group with which he identifies or wishes to identify.

# 6

Implementing Guidance
Information in the Curriculum

### The Curriculum Responsibilities of the Guidance Practitioners

One cannot identify the various responsibilities of the guidance specialist in relation to introducing guidance information and materials in the curriculum without considering the definition of the curriculum. In a school district where a very narrow view of the curriculum is held, that is, where the curriculum is assumed to be the basic text material covered in the various courses of study, the guidance specialist would obviously have a very narrow role to play in integrating guidance information, concepts, and practices in the curriculum. On the other hand, in a school district that encompassed a very broad definition of the curriculum within its educational philosophy, the guidance specialist would enjoy a much more meaningful role and his function would indeed interact with administration and curriculum development.

For the purposes of this monograph we will accept the philosophy that embraces the idea that the curriculum of the school includes all those planned opportunities for learning made available to the student under the sponsorship, direction and supervision of the school. It is necessary to call attention to the fact that within the last five to ten years the role and function of the guidance specialist has greatly increased in scope. Most of the reasons for this increasing importance stem from a rather positive need that has developed in the field of education.

The guidance specialist as coordinator has a very special role to play in the identification of student needs in terms of the demands of today's complex society and he must cooperatively marshall the school staff effort to assist in seeing that these needs can be fulfilled. In other words, the first role of the guidance coordinator in the curriculum is to aid the curriculum specialist in the identification of pupil needs. Unfortunately, when we view the national scene and the various curriculum movements we find that pupil needs have been very generally identified — in fact, too generally identified for actual curriculum development purposes.

This monograph has pointed out that, from what students tell us, as well as from our own observations and surveys of the literature, in the decade in which we live the student needs several things with respect to educational-vocational guidance. First and foremost, students need to have the means for studying vocational opportunities and for studying vocational fields. This is particularly true, as we have seen during this period of great social change in our nation, when suddenly work roles meaningful to the life of our society are opening up to individuals (low income, blacks, women, Mexican-Americans, etc.) that were not previously available to them.

What this means is that students need to have experience in developing a systematic problem-solving approach to finding their place in today's society. That is, they need to have experiences in exploring their interests and talents and relating these aspects of themselves to opportunities that are opening up in the world of work that will enable them to express themselves occupationally. This experience should take place within the framework of their total educational experience. To do this, the student needs to acquire the tools for studying vocational opportunities. He needs to learn the problem-solving methods and skills of inquiry that will prepare him to identify a vocational area that is associated with his talents and interests and that will provide him with personal satisfaction. Concurrently, students need to acquire specific vocational knowledge to prepare them to understand the need for continuous educational training and retraining that they will face during their entire lives.

Specifically, the student will have to know where to find sources of job information, understand the relationship between the economy and certain job fields, know where to find sources of educational information on where he can receive training and retraining not necessarily right away but whenever needed in his life time. These are broad general objectives that have to be woven into the fabric of the curriculum and group guidance activities.

In brief, there must be a basic approach within the framework of the student's educational experience that will provide ways for the student to discover these various aspects of vocational opportunities.

Another student need that is very significant for the field of guidance is the need for pupils to develop a uniqueness of personal interests, hobbies, and activities. Students should learn that they generally fit into a vocational role not only because of what they know or because of what they can do but because of what they are. And, in terms of what they are, this means that more and more educational experience for youth ought to be directed toward the development of attitudes of responsibility, especially toward themselves, attitudes of personal inquiry, and attitudes of unique interests. Further, it seems apparent that the development of these attitudes must be considered aspects of the curriculum. The guidance specialist must insure that there are plenty of opportunities for uniqueness of personal attributes to develop through individualization of instruction, through opportunities for exploration, and through individual and group guidance activities.

Uniqueness of quality of approach to life and work will be the basis upon which a youth will contribute to the society in which he is living. Therefore, uniqueness of life style and quality of personal attributes are representative of the kind of need that the guidance coordinator must recognize and then see that such needs are taken into account in the formation of a curriculum.

It is very apparent that pupils today need to develop broader and broader experiential backgrounds, and this is particularly true of the culturally disadvantaged youngsters. Therefore, to raise the levels of interest of youngsters who have been deprived of important cultural, social, and intellectual experiences, remove constrictions of their horizons, give them the kinds of experiences that will enable them to understand how other people have overcome obstacles and on what basis they have developed motivations to go ahead to do things, improve the quality of their lives, be vocationally important, and so on, it is imperative that every subject area be responsible for setting forth conditions under which increased motivation and personal accomplishment can take place.

Every subject area, whether it be mathematics or science or literature or shop or home economics, has its own career guidance implications for expanding the student's ability to learn more about himself, the subject matter under consideration, and the relationship of the subject matter to future goals and plans.

One major contribution by subject matter specialists to vocational development seems to be in the area of student self-analysis. Each school subject has implications for vocational development whether it be an indication, for example, that (1) competence in this subject is required for success in a given field; or (2) students who enjoy the opportunities this subject provides are discovering an important characteristic about themselves that may in turn have meaning for work; or (3) this subject provides avocational as well as vocational outlets. In addition, there isn't a subject field that doesn't have within its framework national heroes whose lives could be fit subjects for analysis and encouragement as the individual youngster develops.

To assist in this respect, the guidance specialist must keep current with educational trends and with curricula trends so that he can assist the school staff in determining where guidance objectives and concepts should be included within the framework of the available learning experiences.

Chapter 1 of this monograph documented the trend of significant national curriculum movements over the past few years, particularly in science, mathematics, and foreign languages, and to some extent in English. Unfortunately, curriculum efforts have reflected more the theoretical academic learnings that are part of the subject matter fields rather than reflecting a part of the real world in which the larger proportion of our youth typically lives. Although these subject matter improvement efforts have been significantly important in terms of the academic youngster and especially those going into the sciences, they have not been particularly functional when applied to the problems of the non-college bound youth. Success after high school has never depended for this youngster, or for that matter any youngster, solely on particular subjects or courses completed while in school. Rather success after high school has been built upon certain attributes, certain qualities, certain personal abilities and these are aspects of self and behavior that every subject can contribute to.

These include much more than the 3 R's. They include communication skills, attitudes of inquiry and problem solving, the ability to listen discriminately and speak discriminately, and the knowledge and awareness of self and others. Research has indicated that these things seem to be related to post-high school success. Every subject field has an obligation to provide exploratory activities and learning experiences which foster these general attributes and attitudes, and the guidance specialist should be instrumental in suggesting specific content and group, classroom or vocational training activities in which youth might engage to meet these objectives.

## The Importance of the Curriculum Role in Guidance

The role of guidance presently in most schools is destined to be unable to help our youth. The tendency in practice is to reach over into the classroom, draw out the youngster, apply guidance, then put him back in the classroom. This is despite the fact that counselors cannot, I am sure, in good conscience assert that a fifteen minute interview with each student once a year contributes vital guidance services to all. Guidance heretofore has not affected the youngster as he functions within the educational program.

Increasing recognition of the impact of economic, political, and social influence on the life of children and increased knowledge of how children grow and develop is pointing counselors toward the important vocational development implications of implementing guidance in the curriculum — a practice that I believe many counseling and guidance practitioners are not quite ready to face. It is becoming increasingly apparent, however, that although assistance in vocational development is viewed as a guidance function, it cannot be adequately executed by the counselor working alone. It is a joint responsibility — the counselor, teachers, and other school personnel work as a team.

In brief, the points to be made are these:

(1) The counselor's role as a child learns how to make decisions is more important than his role in the area of decision-making.

(2) The educational environment is more important than the counseling interview.

(3) The institutional responsibility properly discharged will be more effective than the contributions of any one counselor.

(4) Parental and teacher involvement is more vital than the counselor's involvement in most cases.

(5) The counselor's willingness to comprehend the etiology of change that is taking place in the social and economic life of his community and the country, and his efforts to see that it is translated into educational processes, may well prevent a greater degree of psychological damage to the student than most of his individual counseling efforts put together.

In conclusion, it is well to note that the overriding value to be gained from implementing guidance in the curriculum seems to lie in what will amount to a continuous, pervasive, impact upon the youth's development while he is still in school; this should have vast implications for improving the quality of his entire life.

# BIBLIOGRAPHY

Bergland, Bruce W. and Krumboltz, John D.: "An Optimal Grade Level for Career Exploration," *The Vocational Guidance Quarterly*, 18, 1969, pp. 29–33.

Borow, Henry: "An Integral View of Occupational Theory and Research." In Henry Borow, ed., *Man In A World at Work*, Houghton Mifflin Co., Boston, 1964, pp. 364–388.

Borow, Henry: "Occupational Information in Guidance Practice Viewed in the Perspective of Vocational Development Theory and Research." In Ann Martin, ed., *Occupational Information and Vocational Guidance for Noncollege Youth*, University of Pittsburgh, Pittsburgh, 1966, pp. 21–34.

Bruner, Jerome S.: "The Cognitive Consequences of Early Sensory Deprivation." In P. Solomon, ed., *Sensory Deprivation*, Harvard University Press, Cambridge, Mass., 1961.

Bushnell, David S.: "An Education System for the 1970's." In Aerospace Education Foundation, *Technology and Innovation in Education*, Frederick A. Praeger, New York, 1968, pp. 121–129.

Cogswell, John F.: "Exploratory Study of Information-Processing Procedures and Computer-Based Technology In Vocational Counseling," Systems Development Corporation, Santa Monica, 1967 (mimeographed).

Combs, A. W. and Syngg, D.: *Individual Behaviors: A Perceptual Approach to Behavior*, Harper, New York, 1959.

Conant, James Bryant: *Slums and Suburbs*, McGraw Hill Book Company, New York, 1961.

Cronbach, Lee J.: "Can a Machine Fit an Applicant to Continuing Education?" *Measurement and Evaluation in Guidance*, 2, 1969, pp. 88–90.

Deutsch, Martin P.: "Facilitating Development in the Preschool Child: Social and Psychological Perspectives," *Merrill Palmer Quarterly*, 10, 1964, pp. 247–263.

Fine, Sidney A.: "A Structure of Worker Functions," *The Personnel and Guidance Journal*, 1955.

Fine, Sidney A.: *The Nature of Automated Jobs and Their Educational and Training Requirements*, Final Report No. HSR-RR-64/6-Ae, prepared for the Office of Manpower Automation and Training, Department of Labor, Contract OAM-3-63, Human Sciences Research, Inc., McLean, Va., 1964.

Fine, Sidney A.: *Guidelines for the Design of New Careers*, Staff paper, W. E. Upjohn Institute for Employment Research, Kalamazoo, Mich., 1967.

Frost, Joe L. and Hawkes, Glenn R., eds.: *The Disadvantaged Child*, Houghton Mifflin Co., New York, 1966.

Gelatt, H. B.: "Decision-making: A Conceptual Frame of Reference for Counseling," *Journal of Counseling Psychology*, 1962, 9, pp. 240–245.

Ginzberg, Eli, Ginsberg, Sol W., Axelrad, S. and Herma, J. L.: *Occupational Choice*, Columbia University Press, New York, 1951.

Goodlad, John I.: *The Changing School Curriculum*, a Report from the Fund for the Advancement of Education, Ford Foundation, New York, 1966.

Gribbons, Warren D. and Lohnes, Paul R.: *Career Development*, Report on Cooperative Research Project Number 5-0088, Regis College, Weston, Mass., 1966.

Hamilton, Jack A. and Krumboltz, John D.: "Simulated Work Experience: How Realistic Should It Be?," *The Personnel and Guidance Journal*, 48, 1969, pp. 39–44.

Jenkins, Jerry A.: "Experimental Design of Counseling Research," A Symposium Paper presented at the 1969 annual meeting of the American Educational Research Association, Indiana State University, 1969 (mimeographed).

Jones, G. Brian and Nelson, Dennis E.: "Approaching a Vocational Education Problem Through Project TALENT — Related Guidance System Components," *The Vocational Guidance Quarterly*, 18, 1970, pp. 187–194.

Katz, Martin: *You; Today and Tomorrow*, 3rd ed., Cooperative Test Division, Educational Testing Service, Princeton, New Jersey, 1959.

Katz, Martin: *Decisions and Values: A Rationale for Secondary School Guidance*, College Entrance Examination Board, New York, 1963, p. 25.

Katz, Martin: "Criteria for Evaluation of Guidance." In Ann Martin, ed., *Occupational Information and Vocational Guidance for Noncollege Youth*, University of Pittsburgh, Pittsburgh, 1966, p. 102.

Keller, Suzanne: "The Social World of the Urban Slum Child: Some Early Findings," *American Journal of Ortho-psychiatry*, 33, 1963, pp. 823–831.

Krathwohl, David R., et al: *Taxonomy of Educational Objectives: Handbook II, Affective Domain*, David McKay Company, Inc., New York, 1966, pp. 20.

Krumboltz, John D.: *Revolution in Counseling: Implications of Behavioral Science*, Houghton Mifflin Company, Boston, 1966.

Magoon, Thomas M.: "An Effective Problem Solving Model for Vocational-Educational Indecision Problems," a paper presented at a Symposium, Guidance Systems and Behavioral Technology, American Educational Research Association, Annual Meeting, Chicago, 1968.

Martin, Ann M.: *Occupational Information and Vocational Guidance for Noncollege Youth,* Edited Proceedings of a Conference held at the University of Pittsburgh, March 11–13, 1966, University of Pittsburgh, Pittsburgh, 1966.

Martin, Ann M.: "A Multimedia Approach to Communicating Occupational Information to Noncollege Youth," Technical Report, U.S.O.E. Contract No. OE 6-85-952, U.S. Department of Health, Education, and Welfare, Office of Education, 1967.

Martin, Ann M.: "Guidance, The Learning Process and Communications Media," *Educational Technology,* 9, 1969a, pp. 46–53.

Martin, Ann M.: "Media and Methodology in Effecting Change," *Educational Technology,* 9, 1969b, pp. 35–38.

Martin, Ann M.: "An Interactive Media for Student and Teacher Growth," *Audiovisual Instruction,* 15, 1970, pp. 53–56.

McLeish, Archibald: *A Continuing Journey,* Houghton Mifflin Co., Boston, 1967.

Miller, A.: "The Bored and the Violent." In J. R. Landis, ed., *Current Perspectives on Social Problems,* Wadsworth Publishing Company, 1966.

Minor, Frank J., Myers, Roger A., and Super, Donald E.: "An Experimental Computer-Based Educational and Career Exploration System," *The Personnel and Guidance Journal,* 47, 1969, pp. 564–572.

Morgan, Robert M. and Bushnell, David S.: "Designing an Organic Curriculum," Staff Paper, Bureau of Research, U.S. Office of Education, Washington, D.C., 1968 (mimeographed).

Ohlsen, Merle M.: "Vocational Counseling for Girls and Women," *Vocational Guidance Quarterly,* 1968, 17, pp. 124–127.

Passow, A. Harry: *Education in Depressed Areas,* Bureau of Publications, Columbia University, New York, 1963.

Perrone, Philip A. and Thrush, Randolph S.: "Vocational Information Processing Systems: A Survey," *The Vocational Guidance Quarterly,* 17, 1969, pp. 255–266.

Riesman, Frank: *The Culturally Deprived Child,* Harper and Row, New York, 1962.

Roeber, Edward C.: "Indirect Exposures and Career Guidance." In Ann Martin, ed., *Occupational Information and Vocational Guidance for Noncollege Youth,* University of Pittsburgh, Pittsburgh, 1966, pp. 91–99.

Rogers, Carl R.: "Toward a Science of the Person." In T. W. Wann, ed., *Behaviorism and Phenomenology: Contrasting Bases for Modern Psychology,* University of Chicago Press, Chicago, 1964, pp. 190–240.

Rosenthal, Robert A. and Bruce, Bernard E.: "The World Across the Street," *Harvard Graduate School of Education Bulletin,* 11, 1966a, pp. 2–24.

Rosenthal, Robert A. et al: *Progress Report* (September 1965–November 1966), Pathways Project, Graduate School of Education, Harvard University, Cambridge, Mass., 1966b.

Rosenthal, Robert A.: "Increasing Sense of Effectiveness Through Media," *Educational Technology*, 9, 1969, pp. 39–45.

Scott, J. W. and Voz, E. W.: "A Perspective on Middle Class Delinquency." In E. U. Voz, ed., *Middle Class Juvenile Delinquency*, Harper and Row, New York, 1967.

Short, James F. and Strodtbeck, Fred L.: *Group Process and Gang Delinquency*, University of Chicago Press, Chicago, 1965.

Skinner, Burrhus F.: *Science and Human Behavior*, Macmillan, New York, 1953.

Super, Donald E.: "A Theory of Vocational Development," *American Psychologist*, 8, 1953, pp. 185–190.

Super, Donald E.: *The Psychology of Careers*, Harper and Row, New York, 1957.

Super, Donald E., Starishevsky, R., Matlin, N., and Jordaan, J. P.: *Career Development: Self Concept Theory*, CEEB Research Monograph No. 4, New York, 1963.

Super, Donald E.: "The Other 50 Percent," Paper presented at the Annual Institute of the Counselors of the Allegheny County Schools, Pittsburgh, Pa., October, 1964.

Tiedemann, David V., and O'Hara, Robert P.: *Career Development, Choice and Adjustment*, College Entrance Examination Board, Princeton, N.J., 1963.

Tiedemann, David V. et al: *Information System for Vocational Decisions*, Annual Report, Harvard Graduate School of Education, Cambridge, Mass., 1967.

Tiedemann, David V.: "The Role of Decision-Making in Information Generation. An Emerging New Generation in Guidance," *ISVD Project Report No. 12*, Graduate School of Education, Harvard University, February, 1968.

Tiedemann, David V.: "Can a Machine Admit an Applicant to Continuing Education," *Measurement and Evaluation in Guidance*, 2, 1969, pp. 69–81.

Tobias, Jerry J.: "Work Activities and Future Goals of the Affluent Suburban Male Delinquent," *The Vocational Guidance Quarterly*, 17, 1969, pp. 293–299.

U.S. Department of Labor: *Manpower Report of the President and a Report on Manpower Requirements, Resources, Utilization and Training*, U.S. Government Printing Office, Washington, D.C., 1966.

Venn, Grant: *Man, Education and Work*, Postsecondary Vocational and Technical Education, American Council on Education, Washington, D.C., 1964.

Wrenn, C. Gilbert: *The Counselor in a Changing World*, American Personnel and Guidance Association, Washington, D.C., 1962.

Yabroff, W.: "Two Experiments in Teaching Decision-Making," Staff paper, Palo Alto Unified School District, California, 1964.

# INDEX

ABCDEFGHIJ— A —765432 1